The Berkshire Studies in European History

GENERAL EDITORS

RICHARD A. NEWHALL
LAURENCE B. PACKARD
SIDNEY R. PACKARD

Berkshire Studies in European History

Under the Editorship of
Richard A. Newhall, Laurence B. Packard
and Sidney R. Packard

THE ENLIGHTENED DESPOTS

BY

GEOFFREY BRUUN

INSTRUCTOR IN HISTORY
NEW YORK UNIVERSITY

NEW YORK
HENRY HOLT AND COMPANY

PREFACE

The college teacher of general European history is always confronted with the task of finding adequate reading for his classes which is neither too specialized and technical nor too elementary. For many topics, including several of the greatest importance, no such material is at the moment available. Moreover, in too many instances, good reading which undeniably does exist is in the form of a chapter in a larger work and is therefore too expensive for adoption as required reading under normal conditions.

The Berkshire Studies in European History have been planned to meet this situation. The topics selected for treatment are those on which there is no easily accessible reading of appropriate length adequate for the needs of a course in general European history. The authors, all experienced teachers, are in nearly every instance actively engaged in the class room and intimately acquainted with its problems. They will avoid a merely elementary presentation of facts, giving instead an interpretive discussion suited to the more mature point of view of college students.

No pretense is made, of course, that these *Studies* are contributions to historical literature in the scholarly sense. Each author, nevertheless, is sufficiently a specialist in the period of which he writes to be familiar with the sources and to have used the latest scholarly contributions to his subject. In order that those who desire to read further on any topic may have some guidance short bibliographies of works in western European languages are given, with particular attention to books of recent date.

Each *Study* is designed as a week's reading. The division into three approximately equal chapters, many of them self-contained and each suitable for one day's assignment, should make the series as a whole easily adaptable to the present needs of college classes. The editors have attempted at every point to maintain and emphasize this fundamental flexibility.

Maps and diagrams will occasionally be furnished with the text when specially needed but a good historical atlas, such as that of Shepherd, is presupposed throughout.

R. A. N.
L. B. P.
S. R. P.

CONTENTS

CONTENTS

THE ENLIGHTENED DESPOTS

CHAPTER I

THE PHILOSOPHY OF THE ENLIGHTENMENT

THE EIGHTEENTH CENTURY

The history of the eighteenth century in Europe is overshadowed by the stirring events that closed it. For the average student the death of Louis XIV in 1715 closes one brilliant and memorable epoch; the calling of the Estates General in 1789 opens the era of the Revolution and Napoleon; but the period between is without a pattern, a confused interval of dynastic intrigues and commercial strife, when the stream of history pursued its languid course towards the unexpected cataract of 1789.

Such an impression of the political history of the century is not altogether unjust. The years from 1715 to 1789 afford for the most part a chronicle of barren diplomacy and abortive wars. French art and arms, which had carried the fame of the Sun King to the corners of Europe, suffered a slow decline under his successor, Louis the Well Beloved. Spain, ruled by a Bourbon after 1701, became a satellite of France and shared her decline. Italy was a collection of petty states under Hapsburg or Bourbon princelings. In Austria the Hapsburgs clung tenaciously to their disunited possessions and waning prestige. Alone of the continental powers, Prussia and Russia made important gains: under the Great Frederick (1740-1786) the Prussian state doubled in area and population; and Russia, pressing forward on the Baltic, in Poland, and along. the Danube, assumed for the first time a prominent rôle in European affairs.

These were developments fraught with important consequences for the nineteenth century, but in the eighteenth they scarcely disturbed the even tenor of the old régime. It was an age of professional diplomats and professional armies; a cynical age when every man was presumed to have his price and the ends sought were commercial gain or dynastic advantage; a formal age of order and etiquette and elegance, under which the wells of the spirit threatened to dry up. A hundred years earlier men had still rushed to battle in the heat of religious fervor, but religion and warfare alike had grown conventionalized. The battalions of the eighteenth century marched and fought like automatons in the grip of a rigid discipline, until they went down to defeat before a horde of ragamuffins shouting the Marseillaise.

Intellectually and culturally the period after the death of Louis XIV in 1715 was still dominated by French influences, a consequence of the ascendency enjoyed by France during his lifetime. Richelieu's dream of making the king supreme in France and France supreme in Europe had come to realization in the glory of the Sun King. Even though the political hegemony of France was undermined by the Peace of Utrecht (1713), Paris remained throughout the eighteenth century the intellectual capital of Europe, and French the language of culture and diplomacy.

Slavishly the courts of Europe set themselves to imitate Parisian arts and manners. French literature was read from St. Petersburg to Lisbon; the French language bound the elegant everywhere into a cosmopolitan society, and the learned into a republic of letters. Beyond the environs of Paris everything ranked as provincial, and the cultured Europeans of other nations acknowledged two motherlands, their own and France.

The plastic mind of Europe was thus stamped with the impress of French genius at a time when such discipline might prove most salutary. In the service of the great writers of the seventeenth century the French tongue had become a medium of marvellous precision and elegance. Montaigne's humanism and rich classical traditions joined to Descartes' genius for organic unity of conception and Malherbe's love of a concise and lucid style had produced a language admirably fitted for the expression of eighteenth century ideas in a form clear, logical, and axiomatic.

Two lines of thought converged in the eighteenth century to form one central strand, on the one hand the belief borrowed from Montaigne that the proper study of mankind is man, on the other the conviction of Descartes that the truth of an idea must be tested by its reasonableness. The philosophy woven from these two lines of thought was rationalism, a faith in reason that was almost a religion, and like a religion counted its prophets, its fanatics, and finally its martyrs. To the rationalists it seemed clear that men were intended by nature to be happy; unhappiness arose for the most part from error or from ignorance. If the rulers of states analyzed all problems in the light of pure reason they would find a cure for all the ills of society. They were physicians who might, by prescribing a rational regimen, restore the body politic to a state of health.

This confident faith in man's power to improve his lot had come into Europe with the Renaissance: there is an interesting comparison to be drawn between the humanists of the sixteenth century and the rationalists of the eighteenth. Like the rationalists, the earlier scholars had also emphasized the need for social reforms, and concurred in assigning to enlightened princes the duty of carrying them out; like the rationalists they prophesied the dawn of a new age, a millennium in which reason would disarm prejudice and make man the master of his destiny. Nor does the parallel end there. For the Utopia of these sixteenth century scholars was still-born into a world soon to be rent by the wars of religious fanaticism; and the eighteenth century idealists—those that survived the Revolution—were destined to see their beloved Republic disappear amid the wars of a new religion of national patriotism.

It is a mistake to think of the French Revolution as introducing new principles into Europe. It only gave dynamic expression to ideas which had been developing throughout the century. But although nearly all its reforms had been projected before, on paper at least, they had been introduced by monarchs and failed to enlist the backing of the people. Several decades before the French revolutionaries declared a war against all kings, the rulers themselves had prepared the way for it by familiarizing their subjects with the idea of reform, and teaching them to desire better government. It is these attempts at social betterment made by the enlightened despots of the old régime, revolutions before the Revolution, that form the subject of this study.

THE INTELLECTUAL TEMPER OF THE AGE

If the leading thinkers of the eighteenth century placed an excessive trust in human reason, they felt this trust to be justified by the achievements of the men of science. Through the use of reason, Newton, in the middle of the previous century, had opened up the heavens and explained the movements of the stars by principles so clear that a child might understand them. Through the use of reason, the wandering comets, which in the Dark Ages had brought terror to the superstitious, had been shown to be harmless visitors, bound, like the stars, by the chains of unalterable law. Even the lightning—hurled, the Church taught, by Satan in his rôle as Prince of the Powers of the Air—had been reduced by reason and experiment to a natural phenomenon: for it, as for the stars and comets, there existed invariable laws, and the human mind, having discovered these, might divert the fury of a bolt by a device as simple as a lightning conductor.

These triumphs of the scientific method led many

writers to predict the dawn of an age wherein man, having discovered the laws of matter, would become the master of nature and of his destiny. It was the dream of Faust. Descartes had declared "that all the things which we very clearly and distinctly conceive are true." This faith in the power of reason to discover truth, and the belief that truth when discovered would never prove self-contradictory or unreasonable, is known as rationalism.

To the rationalists it seemed desirable that they should overhaul every established belief or institution and reconstruct it in the light of pure reason; they held their formula to be a key that would unlock all mysteries. The defect of this optimistic philosophy lay in its first premise. It assumed tacitly that the emotions of the heart, the workings of the mind, the relations of society, and the business of government, could be analyzed by the same methods and with the same ease as the physical sciences. Or, to be more explicit, the rationalists failed to realize that the brilliant mathematical generalizations of the seventeenth century had been achieved in the physical sciences precisely because these were sciences of *measurement;* whereas the branches of knowledge pertaining more nearly to man, as psychology or medicine or anatomy, were still sciences of *classification,* and were not in a state to admit universal generalizations. This weakness of unbridled rationalism was pointed out by the Abbé Mably in 1768. "Is society," he asked ironically, "a branch of physics?" For the consistent rationalist there was only one answer, but it was an answer that committed him to an unqualified materialism.

MATERIALISM

Medieval philosophers, supporting the medieval church, had taught the duality of nature. There was a realm of matter, corrupt and temporary, and a realm of spirit, perfect and eternal. The eighteenth century rationalists reversed this order: with them the world of matter became eternal and unchanging, while the glories of the heavenly kingdom paled like a candle in the sunlight. This exclusive emphasis upon physical phenomena, the belief that nothing exists except matter and that the workings of the mind itself are due wholly to the operation of material agencies, constitutes the body of doctrines known as materialism.

Thinkers of the eighteenth century, steeped in this materialistic philosophy, found it difficult to believe in a world of spirits, or the existence of God. From John Locke (1632-1704) the rationalists had accepted the maxim that nothing existed in the mind that had not come to it through the senses, and the senses could perceive only physical objects. Locke himself, it is true, had not been a consistent materialist, for he found an insecure place in his philosophical system for a belief in God and the immortality of the soul. To Locke's mind, however, God was little more than a First Cause, or Creator of the world, a God who never interfered with the machine he had constructed but left it to run

by itself much like a piece of clock-work. This position of compromise is termed deism. It permitted a
rationalist to accept the existence of God while repudi-
ating all belief in supernatural phenomena, miracles, or
revealed religion.

Such a half-break with theology failed to satisfy the
skepticism of the French mind. It seemed more logical
to the materialists to conceive of matter as indestructible, to accept the world as a perpetual-motion machine, and to dismiss the hypothesis of a Creator
altogether. The physician La Mettrie (1709-1751)
defended these mechanistic views in several works, including his *Histoire naturelle de l'âme* (Natural history
of the soul), and *L'Homme machine* (The man machine). Perhaps the most unattractive picture of the
universe as the abode of dead and soulless matter was
that presented in the *Système de la nature* (The
system of nature), written by the wealthy Baron
D'Holbach (1723-1789). The German poet Goethe
has described in his reminiscences the revulsion which
he felt upon first reading this work, which turned the
face of nature to the hue of a cadaverous spectre.

These writers of the eighteenth century who placed
their trust in human reason and believed that man's
happiness could only be achieved through the spread
of education, or "enlightenment," are known as
philosophes, a French word for which the English term
philosopher is the best though not a very accurate
translation. Not all the *philosophes* were atheists and
materialists. The leader of the school, the great
French publicist Voltaire (1694-1778), remained, like

Locke, a deist. Nor was reason everywhere worshipped without a dissenting voice. The Marquis d'Argenson perceived with alarm the century's pursuit of selfish and rational ends at the expense of the more generous emotions. "We are becoming wholly intellectual beings," he declared. ". . . I predict that this kingdom will perish through the extinction of the faculties which are derived from the heart." In more impetuous fashion Jean Jacques Rousseau gave utterance to the suppressed emotionalism of the period. But Rousseau felt himself to be a lonely iconoclast preaching the claims of the heart to an age which "would rather give feelings to stones than grant a soul to man."

No century is wholly consistent in its thinking, but the eighteenth, despite the protests of such writers as Rousseau, came nearer to the ideal, if it is an ideal, than most. To the *philosophes* faith in the power of reason to improve the lot of mankind was a religion; whatever hindered the spread of enlightenment was an obstacle to be destroyed, an idol to be shattered. Nor did they find any lack of obstacles or of idols. Directly in the path of their progress, clashing with them at almost every point, stood the Roman Catholic Church. Where the rationalists insisted upon man's power to perfect himself through his own efforts, the Church preached his innate depravity and the necessity of redemption. Where the scientists extolled their methods as alone productive of certainties, the Church indicated the Bible and the Fathers as the sources of the highest truth. And where the *philoso-*

phes ridiculed everything which would not support a "reasonable" explanation, the Church proclaimed a belief in miracles, and in such mysteries as the Trinity and the Atonement, necessary for the salvation of the soul.

THE CONFLICT OF RATIONALISM AND RELIGION

"I am happy, Sire," the French scientist.D'Alembert wrote Frederick the Great of Prussia, "to find myself in agreement with Your Majesty as to the hollowness and futility of metaphysics." By metaphysics the enlightened thinkers of the eighteenth century meant all speculations about God and the soul, subjects which, since they regarded them as unknowable, they considered it a waste of time to discuss. There was a growing tendency among all classes to forsake the mysteries of religion for more secular and more congenial studies. The Regent of Orléans carried a copy of Rabelais disguised as a prayer-book to wile away the tedium of a Mass; Madame Roland preferred Plutarch. Court noble and country gentlewoman alike had lost interest in religious observances.

For this indifference the teaching of the *philosophes* was largely responsible. D'Holbach reflected the attitude of a great many rationalists when he wrote in the *Système de la nature*, "The moment a man begins to perplex himself with ideas of God and religion, ideas which he can understand nothing whatever about, his reasoning leads him wildly astray, or else he becomes the victim of sophistries. Yet even when he compre-

hends not a word of what is asserted in such matters
he will credit his teachers with a complete understanding of them; and the latter do not fail to assure
him that the path of certitude is to accept their words
with blind and implicit faith. Should he decline to
believe what he is told, they threaten him with the fury
of a splenetic Shade, and by such an argument, which
begs the whole question at issue, they close everyone's
mouth. . . . Thus the priestly authority settles once
and for all a matter which is of no great profit to
anyone—except the priests."

The power of the Church had waned since the previous century, when Giordano Bruno perished at the
stake, and Galileo, knowing the stars in their courses
would fight on his side, had bowed before the Inquisition.[1] Yet theology still had a subtle power to warp
the reason, and would do so as long as the Church controlled the education of children. Not even the mind
of René Descartes, great rationalist though he was,
had been powerful enough to liberate itself from the
influences that shaped its earliest development. ". . .
Being given assuredly to understand," he wrote, "that
the revealed truths which lead to heaven are above our
comprehension, I did not presume to subject them to
the impotency of my Reason." This allegiance of
Descartes to the teaching of the Church was more than
a mere lip-service prescribed by caution. He never

[1] Giordano Bruno, an Italian philosopher of the Renaissance,
was burned by the Inquisition at Rome in 1600 for maintaining
among other doctrines the theory of Copernicus that the earth
revolves about the sun. Ten years later Galileo (1564-1642)
demonstrated the truth of the Copernican hypothesis by telescopic
observations, but the Inquisition forced him to deny his discoveries.

entirely freed himself from the theological concepts of his Jesuit teachers, and stands, a Janus-figure, at the gateway of modern philosophy.

All such lingering reverence for religious dogmas it was the aim of the rationalists to destroy by ridicule. Thus, in imitation of the earlier philosophers, they still prefaced metaphysical discussions with a preliminary obeisance to Mother Church; but with Voltaire the gesture is ironical. "I will not . discuss our own [religion] here," he wrote in his Philosophical Dictionary. "It alone is good, necessary, demonstrable. . . . But if it were possible for the human mind to conceive a second (I will not say at all approaching ours, but better than all other creeds of the world together) what would that religion be like? Would it not urge us to worship the 'Supreme Being, unique, infinite, eternal, who created the world? . . . Would it not reject the dogmas invented by pride which are subjects of endless disputations, and teach instead a pure morality about which there could be no dispute? . . . Would it not enjoin us to serve our neighbors through love of God, instead of persecuting and butchering them to his greater glory? And would not such a faith, which by tolerance towards all could earn the goodwill of all, be alone capable of uniting mankind into a nation of brothers?"

The high water mark of success in the rationalist assault upon the Church was reached in 1773 when Pope Clement XIV was persuaded to suppress the Society of Jesus. There were several reasons why the Jesuits should have been singled out for attack. Organized first in 1540 they had made themselves the "spear-head" of the Catholic or Counter Reformation, and had become the most powerful single factor in checking heresy and defending the papal authority. The society exacted the highest degree of discipline and obedience from its members, for its founder, Ignatius Loyola, planned that his followers should be soldiers and, if need be, martyrs of Christ. He prayed that persecution should be their lot and they earned it by an unflinching devotion to the interests of the papacy and an unremitting warfare against heretics and freethinkers. In the eighteenth century the enemies of the Jesuits were more numerous than ever before. Even the Popes were suspicious of their powers, and members of other religious orders resented their independence and the secrecy of their organization. Their great influence, because it was often exerted through hidden channels, appeared to their enemies peculiarly sinister. Kings suspected them of encouraging the people to believe it was legitimate to murder a tyrant; the people attributed unpopular edicts of the princes to the influence of Jesuit confessors. To the *philosophes* with their love of religious freedom the Jesuits were a symbol of that spirit of dogmatism in the Church against which above all else they were fighting.

In France the growing hatred of the Jesuits resulted in their expulsion from the kingdom in 1764. Although the members were pledged to poverty they had long indulged in commercial ventures which brought the Society into discredit, for they used their privileges, especially in the American colonies, to extend their trading activities, and amassed enormous wealth. Yet when, in 1755, a Jesuit mission in Martinique became bankrupt, leaving debts of two million *livres*, the Society repudiated any responsibility. The resulting litigation in the French courts excited an extraordinary animosity against the Jesuits until in 1764 they were driven out of France. Their expulsion from Spain and Portugal is recorded elsewhere.[1] Finally, in 1773, Pope Clement XIV was coerced into revoking their charter, and the dissolution of the Order was hailed as a victory by leaders of the Enlightenment throughout Europe. In their taste of power the rationalists showed little compassion for the deported fathers; almost alone Frederick the Great of Prussia displayed concern over their sufferings and offered them a refuge in his dominions. "As for me, heretic that I am," he wrote D'Alembert when he heard the Order was to be scattered, "I shall take the credit of collecting the débris in Silesia, and not add to their misfortunes."

NATURAL RELIGION

The religious institutions which the *philosophes* regarded so lightly were the dogmatic shells of a burned out faith. They lived in an age bankrupt of idealism and of spiritual values. Religious enthusiasm they dismissed as bad form. Had they been capable of understanding the flame which had burned in John Huss or Francis of Assisi, they could not have planned so casu-

[1] See Chap. III.

ally to remodel rituals and bank the fires of faith.
Because the forces of the heart left them unmoved they
took no account of them. Thus they failed to gauge
the explosive indignation of the bourgeoisie, to divine
the dumb anger of the peasants, or the latent spirit of
nationalism that was to make and unmake a Napoleon.
They played with these sleeping passions as carelessly
and audaciously as Said the Fisherman played with the
bottle imprisoning the genie.

At heart they were not radicals. Utopia, to these
intellectuals, was a replica of eighteenth century society in which they were to be freed from all vexatious interference and promoted to a more honorable
station. To perfect and perpetuate the old régime, not
to destroy it, was their aim; and their revolutionary
criticism was designed, paradoxically enough, to make
society more static and more conservative. A tranquil
civilization, such as they imagined the Chinese to be, in
which sages were honored and the masses remained
contented with their lot, appeared to them ideal.

In such a society, the society of which they dreamed,
religious teaching was to become a civic affair, the
handmaid of good government, spreading a spirit of
harmony among all classes. Europe's warring sects
were to be supplanted by a religion of nature which
would unite the human race in the rites of a simple
cult. To the rationalists it seemed clear that the Supreme Being, who had established harmonious principles to govern the movements of the farthest star,
could never have intended the relations of men to remain in chaos. Left to itself, they felt assured, the

human reason could soon discover the laws of social harmony. A new generation, born into a world purged of sectarian controversy and priestly machinations, should know the truth and the truth would make them free. Since the child's mind was a *tabula rasa* it would accept the principles of natural religion because of their sweet reasonableness. Then all men would live together in amity, recognizing the right of each to life, liberty, and the pursuit of happiness. They held these truths to be self-evident.

THE OLD RÉGIME

Everywhere the burden of the old régime weighed like an incubus upon Europe. The peasantry, though they were still oppressed by the obligations of feudalism, had foregone its benefits. As the national monarchies developed kings had increased their authority until they curbed the feudal nobles; but for the common people this change meant only the advent of a new and more efficient master. Wealth and power remained in the hands of the few. In France, with a population of twenty-five million, only one person in a hundred belonged to the "privileged" classes. The rich devoured the poor, as the Marquis de Mirabeau [1] said, "like pikes in a pond." What the royal tax-collector overlooked the feudal lord was swift to seize. For though the nobles stood between the people and the

---

[1] Victor Riqueti, Marquis de Mirabeau (1715-1789) was a French writer and political economist. He is not to be confused with his more famous son, Gabriel Honoré Riqueti, Comte de Mirabeau (1749-1791), the great orator of the French Revolution.

crown, it was only, in the bitter phrase of one writer, "as the hounds are between the hunter and the hare."

The peasants, the most hopeless victims of this system, were too crushed by their misfortunes to protest; it was the middle classes that raised most loudly the cry of social injustice. Wealthy bourgeois who envied the nobility; merchants whose profits were destroyed by illogical tariffs or swallowed up in endless lawsuits; journalists whose books were burned by stupid censors—all read Voltaire and shared his indignation at the existing régime. They demanded—and it was a bourgeois platform—equitable taxation, simplified laws, intellectual liberty, and religious toleration.

For such reforms there was a genuine practical need: they should have been attempted for the sake of governmental efficiency if for no other reason. But the privileged classes naturally opposed any change, defending the established methods as sacrosanct. The abuses had been hallowed by tradition; to destroy them it was necessary to destroy first the reverence with which they were regarded. For such a task Voltaire and his disciples were peculiarly fitted. Whenever they discovered some pious fraud or miscarriage of justice they delighted to make a public scandal of it, to hold its perpetrators up to ridicule and laugh them out of court. Every grievance against the Church which came to their attention, every blunder of officialdom, provided them with an opportunity for turning loose the terrific stream of their ridicule, that astringent satire with which they planned to cleanse the Augean stables of Europe.

But if, as Professor Whitehead has said, men cannot live on bread alone, still less can they live on disinfectants. Ridicule might weaken abuses but it did not destroy them. Arguments had to be met by arguments, authorities by authorities. So to the established order, and the force of tradition, the rationalists opposed a natural order, and the force of reason. Like all astute reformers they pretended that their program offered no new departure but a return to first principles. The government had grown corrupt, the laws were in confusion, virtue had decayed, religion was sunk in ritual. It was necessary to "purify society," to "destroy the cancerous abuses," to "cut off the gangrened limb." Then the body politic, under the direction of skillful physicians, would return to a state of health.

On every side the *philosophes* found examples of inefficiency, confusion, devotion to precedent, whereas what they worshipped above all things was enlightenment—clarity, method, order. Too often the governments which were maintained to regulate the affairs of nations could not organize their own departments. Finance ministers cast up the accounts of a state with a slovenliness that would have ruined a third-rate banking house. Their budgets and balance sheets were often matters of pure guess-work; they had no accurate data for calculating the resources of a nation, no adequate means for collecting the taxes, no method for regulating the expenditure.

Such conditions the critics of government denounced quite rightly as irrational. When they demanded that the institutions of society should be reorganized in accordance with natural laws, they were only voicing in borrowed philosophic terms the desire of all sane men for greater efficiency in the management of the state. The reasoning of philosophers about nature and society was harmless enough in itself and little likely to disturb the established order. Indeed, many of the political writers of the eighteenth century preferred to confine themselves entirely to brilliant generalizations, and to leave specific grievances alone. But in an age so full of abuse and discontent there were plenty of bolder minds ready to give to airy nothings a local habitation and a name, and to convert abstract formulas about natural law and natural right into sharp-edged weapons for hacking at the tree of privilege and the chains of superstition. No handful of intellectuals, however busily they sowed the wind, could have stirred to its depths a satisfied and prosperous society; but the people of Europe in the eighteenth century were few of them either prosperous or happy.

THE CONFUSION OF JURISTIC AND SCIENTIFIC LAW

The key to eighteenth century political thinking is the idea of natural law. Behind the variety of nature the *philosophes* felt was a rational order, a kind of mathematical pattern. The idea was not new. "God geometrizes," Plato said, and he sought for reality in certain ultimate Ideas pre-existent in the mind of God—"Types, whose earthly copies were the foolish broken things we knew." It had been a precept of the Stoics likewise that "Nature has established rational principles for all that is": the idea, embedded in the philosophy of Roman law had been borrowed by Aquinas and by Dante after him. But in the eighteenth century the concept took, on a sudden, new vitality. For reason, following the inductive method, had begun to uncover these natural laws and to find in them a beauty, a simplicity, a self-sufficiency beyond all expectations. Remained only the task of reconciling life to its pattern and remodelling human institutions in accord with nature's pre-established harmony.

Since the reorganization of society in accordance with these underlying principles could best be brought about by effective legislation, the rationalists turned their attention to the problem of legal reform. The need for a single simplified code of law in each state had been evident since the sixteenth century, yet in France alone, before the Revolution, justice was administered according to three hundred and sixty different codes. No one could determine where the jurisdiction of manorial courts ended, where that of the provincial *parlements* began, or what pretext might authorize the intervention of the royal *intendants*. So justice lagged and lawyers flourished, while the business of life was tied up by a mass of contradictory legislation and conflicting decisions.

For all this the *philosophes* had a simple solution. The function of the legislator was not to make laws but to discover them. Men in society no less than bodies in space were subject to rational principles; the formulation of these was to be the miracle which would bring harmony out of chaos. Since the new legal formulas would possess the same lucidity and command the same acceptance as the axioms of Euclid, they would establish in the affairs of government a mathematical precision. This miscalculation, this confusion of juristic with scientific law, could only have occurred in a century obsessed, like the eighteenth, with the triumphs of mathematics. It made society, as Mably had pointed out, a branch of physics.

The codification of a new table of law was thus to be the first step in the *philosophes'* program of reform. These laws were to be few in number, based upon natural principles, and expressed in such simple language that the wayfaring man, though a fool, might not err therein. The more optimistic theorists even hoped that such a code, like the legislation of the Utopians, would possess in itself a rectifying quality, so that the citizens enjoying its benefits "could not choose but be good." They believed that the institution of wise laws would produce a spirit of harmony and coöperation in society, an improved morale, unique and unmistakable, which they distinguished by the term Virtue, and which Plato had defined as "a kind of health and beauty and good condition of the soul." In the nineteenth century a similar hope inspired many democratic leaders to dream that universal manhood suffrage would harmonize the interests of all classes and build a bridge to Utopia. It is a perennial ideal.

Stripped of its Utopian elements the plan for judicial reform, like those projected in education, in agriculture, in sanitation, possessed excellent possibilities. There was, however, another problem more pressing than these. The sinews of government, as of war, are sound finances; the primary problem of statecraft, most absorbing to king and people alike, was the task of securing the economic welfare of the nation. To discharge its functions a government had to command an adequate revenue; to meet the necessary taxation the people had to be rendered reasonably prosperous. This vital connection between economics and government was developed into a philosophy towards the middle of the eighteenth century by a group of French thinkers who have become famous in history as the *économistes* or Physiocrats.

THE PHYSIOCRATS

The term *physiocrate* did not come into general use until the nineteenth century; for themselves the followers of Quesnay preferred the title *économistes.* But physiocracy, implying as it does government according to natural order, expresses so much more definitely the central doctrine of this school that it has superseded the earlier term.

François Quesnay (1694-1774) was court physician to Louis XV, but his chief interest lay in economic and agricultural problems. In 1756 and 1757 he contributed to the *Encyclopédie* of Diderot two articles on agricultural subjects wherein he set forth the principles of a new system of political philosophy. His ideas were adopted with enthusiasm by the young Dupont de Nemours, who, believing with the faith of an acolyte that the true method of reforming society had been revealed at last, sought to popularize Quesnay's system in a work which he published under the ambitious title *De l'origine et du progrès d'une science nouvelle* (On the origin and progress of a new science).

At the basis of Quesnay's thinking was a belief in natural order. "Laws," he affirmed, "are rules of justice, morality, and conduct, applicable to all and each. Men and governments never made them, nor ever could; they can only recognize them as conforming to the supreme reason which governs the universe." In the discovery and application of these natural principles lay the secret of reforming society. "There is one essential route," wrote Dupont de Nemours, "by which we can approach, as nearly as it is possible to do, to the problem of human association and the formation of political bodies. There is a natural order, necessary and universal, which determines the basic and constitutional laws of all societies . . . an order which can never be forsaken without inviting the dissolution of society and the complete destruction of the human race."

The fame of the Physiocrats did not consist, however, in the belief that nature held a pattern of which man-made laws were supposed to be a replica. Such ideas were the common property of almost all eighteenth-century thinkers. The peculiar success of Quesnay, according to his followers, lay in the fact that he had *discovered* and *isolated* those basic laws of society upon which all else depended. He was the Newton of the social system, the originator of that "new science" which Dupont de Nemours was ready to celebrate.

If genuine, the triumph of this ugly little man, whom his disciples likened to Socrates, was an unparalleled achievement, and all Europe was ready to attend. But the results proved disappointing. Quesnay published some general maxims of government and accompanied them by an economic chart, but the maxims lacked that compelling simplicity which natural laws were supposed to possess; and the *Tableau économique*, even though he supplemented it by seven appendices and the Marquis de Mirabeau explained it in three ponderous volumes, remained incomprehensible to most readers. Voltaire poured ridicule upon the members of the school; the Abbé Mably opposed to their conception of a state his own fantastic and idealized Sparta; and theorists who preferred to amuse themselves with the construction of airy Utopias shrank from the labor of grappling with the abstruse economic formulas upon which the Physiocrats based their philosophy.

It is, in fact, as economic theorists rather than as political philosophers that the Physiocrats deserve consideration. Though many of their most cherished axioms were wrong, even a wrong axiom may have its uses as a weapon of destruction in the hands of a reformer. Eighteenth century writers on political economy, such as Richard Cantillon who died in 1734, and Vincent de Gournay (1712-1759), had ventured to attack the prevailing mercantilist or bullionist theory of trade. This theory taught that to remain prosperous a state should preserve a favorable balance of trade, that is, it should make the value of its exports exceed that of its imports. The excess value of the goods exported, it was held, must then be paid for in gold by the country receiving them, thus directing a steady stream of bullion to the state which successfully adhered to mercantilist principles. Against this system the Physiocrats, following in the footsteps of Cantillon and Gournay, raised a number of objections. The wealth of a state, they insisted, could not be increased by accumulating gold, but only by the mass of its agricultural and mineral products unconsumed in the process of production. To this annual increase in the sum of raw material available for human use they applied the term *produit net* (net profit), and they made it the basis of a new theory of political economy.

The economic teaching of the Physiocrats appeared fantastic to a majority of their contemporaries and exerted little influence in France before the Revolution. Across the Channel, however, the Scotsman Adam Smith (1723-1790) was analyzing the same problems, and the publication in 1776 of his famous treatise "An Inquiry into the Nature and Causes of the Wealth of Nations" was in many respects a vindication of physiocratic theories. Like the pupils of Quesnay, Smith condemned mercantilism and exalted labor as the source of wealth and the standard of value; but he was less obsessed than they by prepossessions regarding natural law and other abstract philosophical principles, and his writings had a wider influence and a greater value than theirs.

Almost all the *philosophes* were distinguished by an intolerant assurance and a prodigious conceit which made them at times more than a little wearisome; but the Physiocrats were perhaps the most dreary of the lot. Monarchs like Frederick II of Prussia (1740-1786) or Catharine II of Russia (1762-1796), who understood the difficulties of practical administration, sometimes listened with a strained patience to the pedantic lectures of these philosophers whom they, and all Europe, delighted to honor. "They sing their own praises," confessed Gustavus III of Sweden (1771-1792), "with as much complacency as ever their admirers could do." And Frederick wrote in 1774, "Diderot is at St. Petersburg, where the Czarina has overwhelmed him with honors; but they say that his arguments fill her with weariness for he does nothing but repeat the same things over and over again." When Catharine was planning a new code of laws for the Russian people she invited Mercier de la Rivière to her court, but one encounter with the dogmatism of the physiocratic mind sufficed to satisfy her. "Can you tell me, Sir," she asked, "the best way to govern a state well?"—"There is only one, Madame," replied the pupil of Quesnay, "it is to be just, that is, to maintain order and to enforce the laws."—"But on what basis should the laws of an empire repose?"—"On one alone, Madame, the nature of things and men."—"Exactly, but when one wishes to give laws to a people, what rules indicate most surely the laws which suit it best?"— "To give or make laws, Madame, is a task which God has left to no one. Ah, what is man, to think himself capable of dictating laws to beings whom he knows not, or knows so imperfectly? And by what right would he impose laws upon beings whom God has not placed in his hands?"—"To what, then, do you reduce the science of government?"—"To study well, to recognize and manifest, the laws which God has so evidently engraven in the very organization of man when he gave him existence. To seek to go beyond this would be a great misfortune and a destructive undertaking." [1]

ENLIGHTENED DESPOTISM

As champions of individual liberty the Physiocrats deplored all arbitrary methods of government; but they believed none the less that the central authority of the state had to be preserved. Power might be a good or an evil thing according to the use that was made of it, but it could not be dispensed with nor dissipated. "There should be one sovereign authority superior to all the individuals of a society," Quesnay had declared. "The idea of several authorities in the same state," added Dupont de Nemours, "suggests nothing less than an absurdity." To these philosophers it seemed better that the promulgation of the laws should be entrusted to a monarch rather than to a legislature; for if all the legislators thought alike, one head would do as well as many; whereas if the legislators differed, it would prove that they were not equally enlightened. So with the exception of one or

[1] Thiebault, *Souvenirs de vingt ans de séjour à Berlin,* 2nd ed. III, pp. 167-68. Quoted in H. Higgs, *The Physiocrats,* p. 88.

two of their number—Mirabeau, Morellet—the Physiocrats agreed in favoring that form of government which is known as enlightened despotism.

The word despot, however, they wished to strip of all ugly connotations. The true despot ought to be the servant of his people, exercising his power solely for their good, and recognizing their welfare as his own. There were two methods by which society might be regenerated. One, a slow and laborious method, depended upon the gradual spread of enlightenment until it reached all classes and individuals in a state. The second, promising swifter results, might be set in action if a wise prince, a modern Lycurgus, instituted at one sweep the necessary laws of social harmony. An enlightened ruler, provided his power were adequate, could reorganize and revivify the life of a nation by a few well-reasoned edicts, and thus earn the gratitude of his people.

Such a prince could make the title of despot glorious. Since his ordinances would, on their own merits, win the acceptance of all right-thinking men, they would scarcely require the backing of his absolute authority. "Euclid," wrote Mercier de la Rivière, "is the true type of despot. The geometrical axioms which he has transmitted to us are genuine despotic laws; in them the legal and the personal despotism of the legislator are one and the same thing, a force evident and irresistible; and for that reason the despot Euclid has for centuries exercised his unchallenged sway over all enlightened peoples."

For the first time in history the art of government

might be raised to an exact science, and the affairs of
men regulated, it was hoped, with perfect order and
efficiency. An opportunity unique and enviable was
offered the monarchs of the eighteenth century: it was
to be their privilege to reorganize society in accordance
with the new discoveries. "It is an obligation laid upon
sovereigns," proclaimed Dupont de Nemours, "to pro-
mulgate by positive ordinances the natural and essential laws of the social order."

Thus royal despotism in Europe entered its third and
final stage. The idea had won acceptance that kings
existed for the benefit of their people, not the people
for the benefit of the king. In the Reformation era a
ruler like Philip II imposed his will and his religion
upon his subjects, and held himself responsible to
God alone. This period of confessional absolutism, as
Professor Koser has termed it, was followed in the
seventeenth century by the brilliant, courtly despotism
of Louis XIV, well suggested by the motto *l'état c'est
moi*. But the eighteenth century introduced a new pattern of kingship, and the magnificence of the Grand
Monarch was eclipsed by the restless figure of Frederick the Great, wielding his unlimited authority, not
as a divine right, but as a trust devolving upon him as
the first servant of the state.

Frederick was the most brilliant and the most successful of the eighteenth century despots, and he served
as a model for his contemporaries. Throughout Europe
earnest and ambitious princes strove to imitate him,
and to apply the principles of the Enlightenment to secure the welfare of their subjects. Too scant a justice

served in...
atone for the mistakes their ancestors ...
in five: the eighteenth century was, in Lord Acton's
phrase, "the monarchs' age of repentance."

Young rulers prepared themselves for the duties of
kingship by reading the works of the *philosophes*, en-
thusiastically, but it is to be feared, uncritically. Furthermore, they corresponded with each other in order
to compare their reform programs. Setting aside minor
differences they expected to find the principles of good
government of universal application and they strove to
see who should first discover and apply them. "Here is
the summary," Dupont de Nemours had suggested
modestly in closing his *Origine et progrès d'une science
nouvelle*—"Here is the summary of that teaching
which, in accordance with the nature of man, reveals
the laws essential to a government made for man and,
proper to man in all climates and all lands; to the society which has existed in China these four thousand
years under the Tropic of Cancer, and to that government which the genius of a great empress is raising
even now for the happiness of her subjects amid the
frozen wastes of the North. . . ."

This optimistic passage was penned by Dupont de

_____ ___y Roman Emperor and
co-regent with his mother Maria Theresa, was preparing a list of extraordinary reforms against the day when
he should assume sole authority in the Hapsburg
dominions. The Spanish people were enjoying the
enlightened rule of Charles III, while in Portugal
the reforming minister Pombal was at the height of his
power. It seemed as if a single generation might wit-
ness the reconstruction of European society. "There
is no prince in Europe," wrote Diderot confidently,
"who is not also a philosopher."

THE EIGHTEENTH CENTURY UTOPIA

It is an easy matter to point out that the ideal state
projected by these theorists was an impossible one.
Philosophers are for the most part bookish men, averse
to all forms of tumult or violence, and over-regardful
of that decency than which is life less dear. The society planned by the *philosophes* was to be orderly,
harmonious, and static; since beyond perfection there
can be no advance, they omitted the elements of conflict and progress and evolution. Even when they
urged a return to nature, they never envisaged her in
a savage or primitive mood. What they had in mind
was a landscape of Watteau—a sylvan Arcady where

storms never ventured, and all uncouth passions and destructive forces were softened by the touches of a deft technique.   Through the use of some similar magic—a few swift strokes, a little dexterous foreshortening—they planned to resolve the conflicts of society into a picture of order and elegance.   Then they would lead a regenerate humanity back to Arcadia— an Arcadia as timeless as a dream or a painting, from which they had banished all unreasoned impulses and infinite horizons.

The doctrinaire mind always betrays itself in the attempt to wrench reality into agreement with an arbitrary pattern.   Disquieted at times by the cold perfection of their ideal state, the *philosophes* sought to fit humanity into the picture, only to behold their categories crack beneath the strain.   From this predicament they escaped—in theory at least—by the dogma of human perfectibility.   The children of the future, better educated, purged of ancient habits and prejudices, would know how to venerate the philosophy of enlightenment; with a new generation, stamped with the matrix of perfected institutions, mankind would come into its heritage.

When the Revolution threw down the gates and a turbulent humanity poured into Arcadia the whole framework collapsed like the theatrical setting it was. Few figures in history are more tragic than the idealists of 1793 and 1794, who sought like Robespierre to hold together the ruins of a syllogistic paradise, or learned with the Girondins that the genie of revolution, once unloosed, can not be persuaded back into its bottle.

These men could not live their dream, but they did not hesitate to die for it; after them came Napoleon, to pour contempt upon the ideologists, and to announce that the romance of the Revolution was over.

Perhaps the most charming picture that exists of the eighteenth century Utopia is to be found in the memoirs of Marmontel. "I had the happiness," he wrote in his last years, "to be born in a place where the inequalities of rank or fortune were scarcely felt. A few possessions, a little trade or industry, supplied the needs of almost all the inhabitants of the tiny village in the Limousin where first I saw the day. There a comfortable livelihood took the place of wealth, and everyone enjoyed an independent existence dignified by some useful occupation. . . . Above the village—itself a verdant island circled by the river and enlivened by the stir and clatter of its mill—stood a small forest alive with birds; . . . and not far distant lay our tiny farm, where, prone in the shadow of the trees, I used to read my Virgil. . . ."

Utopia, being of the stuff that dreams are made on, survived the fury and disillusionment of the Revolution, and emerged again from the turbulent years shining and indestructible as ever. But this time it lay in the past. As the young men who had seen visions became old men dreaming dreams, Europe of the old régime, softened by distance, took on the colors of the lost Arcadia. "Only those who were alive before 1789," conceded the aging Talleyrand, "know how sweet life can be."

CHAPTER II

FREDERICK II, JOSEPH II AND CATHARINE II

With the death of Frederick William I, on May 21, 1740, the throne of Brandenburg-Prussia passed to a young prince, twenty-eight years of age, who had been his father's despair. The fondness of the youthful Frederick for such impractical pursuits as flute-playing and French versification had driven Frederick William to employ Spartan severities in an effort to reform his son. He drilled him doggedly in the details of civil and military administration, left him a well-filled treasury, and died with the hope that Frederick, despite his effeminate inclinations, might prove not wholly a disgrace to the House of Hohenzollern.

The death of Frederick William was followed five months later by that of the Hapsburg emperor, Charles VI. The House of Austria at this period ruled over some twenty-five million people; in conjunction with its great rival, the House of Bourbon, it controlled the destinies of Europe. The Hapsburgs were masters of the Danube Valley, Lombardy, Suabia, and the Austrian Netherlands. The Bourbons ruled France, Spain, Naples, and the Two Sicilies. In the predominance of these two dynasties the young Frederick recognized a danger to the smaller states of Europe. A third power was needed, he felt, to counter-balance the other two; and he prepared to strike the audacious blows by which he crippled the House of Austria and raised Prussia, with her five million inhabitants, to the rank of a first rate power.

Charles VI left no male heir to the Austrian lands, but he managed to secure from all the courts of Europe a guarantee that his daughter Maria Theresa should succeed to the Hapsburg claims. But Frederick, ignoring the Pragmatic Sanction to which Prussia had been a signatory, invited France and Bavaria to join him in seizing the lands of the young and inexperienced Empress-Queen. For his own share Frederick coveted the province of Silesia; having secured it by a swift campaign, he made peace with Maria Theresa at Breslau in 1742. Then, fearing that Austria might recover too rapidly from her misfortunes, he rejoined France and Bavaria in the field, only to desert them a second time by the Peace of Dresden in 1745. "Happy are they," he wrote after extricating himself with his spoils for the second time, "who, having secured their own safety, can tranquilly regard the embarrassment of others."

FREDERICK'S REFORMS

The reëstablishment of peace between Prussia and Austria in 1745 left Frederick free to turn his restless mind to problems of civil administration. Rising before six in the morning, he spent the hours of the forenoon laboring over the business of state. No department of government escaped his scrutiny and no detail appeared too petty for his attention. While still in his early thirties he had proved himself one of the most brilliant generals of the age; he was now to win equal fame as an exponent of the form of government which is known as enlightened despotism. The most influential writings of the *philosophes* on this subject did not appear until after 1750, but before that date Frederick had recognized many of the abuses they were later to attack and had anticipated the remedies they recommended for them. While his services in organizing the administration of the Prussian state cannot here be discussed at length, the present account would be incomplete without at least a short summary of his reforms.

The manner in which Frederick had utilized the military resources of Prussia in the War of the Austrian Succession revealed his powers of decision, his skill in choosing able subordinates, and his love of efficiency. These qualities served him quite as well 'n the duties of civil administration. His constant supervision rendered the Prussian bureaucracy the most efficient in Europe. To his interest in legal reform was due the reorganization of the judicial system and the compilation of the first unified code of German law. The Berlin Academy of Sciences was a matter of particular pride to him, and he induced the French scientist Maupertuis to accept the presidency of that body. The system of elementary education benefited from his interest in the field of public instruction. He tolerated every form of religious belief, granted his subjects complete freedom of speech, and a considerable degree of liberty to the press. All these reforms, however, were instituted as the regulations of an autocrat, and never as concessions to popular demands. No monarch was ever more imperious than Frederick in maintaining his royal authority. The freedom of speech which he encouraged among his associates had definite limits; Voltaire himself, when visiting the Prussian king, was reprimanded for an incautious remark. The privilege of criticism was one which Frederick reserved for himself, nor did he hesitate to indulge it on occasion with the most merciless sarcasm.

FISCAL AND MILITARY IMPROVEMENTS

By careful economies in the management of the state Frederick was able to devote a large part of the revenue to agricultural and industrial enterprises. Thousands of acres of waste land reclaimed by a system of drainage canals were placed under cultivation; and the king, in his visits to all parts of his dominions, regulated old industries, instituted new ones, and infused into the affairs of local administration something of his own energy and love of order.

The Prussian army remained to the close of his life the instrument in which Frederick reposed his chief trust for the safety of his state. From 80,000 he increased it during his reign to nearly 200,000 men; he wrote treatises on the science of warfare for the instruction of his generals; and his death was hastened by a chill contracted during a military review. To understand the faith which he placed in a well-disciplined army, a faith which he had found to be justified, it is necessary to turn back to the events of the Seven Years' War when the courage of the Prussian soldiers and the skill of their king were all that saved Prussia from being divided among the neighboring powers.

THE SEVEN YEARS' WAR

The empire of the Hapsburgs, like a falling house that never falls, had surprised its enemies by weathering all adversities, and when the War of the Austrian Succession ended in 1748 Maria Theresa had won back all her hereditary dominions except Silesia. Frederick watched the recovery of Austria with apprehension. He knew that Maria Theresa would never forget Silesia and that he might have to fight again to retain the province which he had snatched, for the duel between Hapsburgs and Hohenzollerns for leadership in the German lands had barely commenced. During the eight years of peace that followed, from 1748 to 1756, while Frederick was reorganizing the Prussian state Maria Theresa likewise attempted to introduce a greater degree of centralization and efficiency into the administration of the Hapsburg domains. As Empress of Austria, and Queen of Bohemia and Hungary, she ruled an empire possessed of five times the resources of Prussia. She refused to regard Silesia as irretrievably lost.

Throughout its history the House of Austria has been weakened by the fact that the Hapsburg possessions could never be forged into a national state. The subjects of Maria Theresa spoke ten different languages and represented as many nationalities; however deep their loyalty to the Empress-Queen they felt no common Austrian patriotism. Furthermore, the various provinces possessed local privileges which rendered the centralization of power in the hands of the monarch a difficult policy to pursue. Maria Theresa was careful to respect the prejudices of her subjects; cautious and diplomatic by nature, she feared to attempt a reconstruction of the government from its foundations. Her reforms, in their incompleteness, have been aptly compared to the addition of modern wings to a feudal castle.

These circumstances made it impossible for Austria to rival the bureaucratic efficiency of the Prussian state, but Maria Theresa proved more fortunate than Frederick in securing allies. Frederick's audacious ambition to build up a third power capable of exercising an equal share with the Bourbons and Hapsburgs in the management of European affairs drove those rival dynasties together. In 1756 Austria and France forgot an enmity dating from the fifteenth century and signed a treaty of alliance at Versailles; but although Maria Theresa gained one ally she lost another. In the War of the Austrian Succession she had enjoyed the benefit of English aid, but Great Britain was engaged in a colonial struggle with France and could not be expected to support Austria in her new course. Consequently, while from 1740 to 1748 Austria and England had fought Prussia and France, from 1756 to 1763 Austria and France were to fight Prussia and England. The change in Austrian policy which brought about this new alignment of the Great Powers is known as the "Diplomatic Revolution."

With France won over to the Austrian side, a result largely due to Maria Theresa's skillful minister, Count Kaunitz, the coalition against Frederick seemed complete. Austria, Russia, France, Saxony, and Sweden, acting together, could hardly fail to crush any resistance Frederick might offer; the allies foresaw an easy victory, to be followed by the dismemberment of the Prussian kingdom. As the plot matured Frederick learned through secret channels of the fate that was being prepared for him. In 1756 he came to an agreement with the only possible ally that remained, and signed the Convention of Westminster with Great Britain; then, rather than wait until the Russians, Austrians and French were ready to attack him, he forced them into the field prematurely by a sudden descent upon Saxony, seized the resources of that state, and compelled its army to swear allegiance to himself. To the Saxon commander's protest that history afforded no precedent for such an act, Frederick responded that he prided himself upon being somewhat original.

In the seven years that followed, this young prince whom his father had once planned to disinherit proved himself the most brilliant general of his age, and baffled his opponents by a defence among the most desperate and successful that history describes. In 1761 Great Britain withdrew her subsidies; and in the succeeding year, when the game must have grown too desperate to last, Frederick was saved by the death of his implacable enemy, the Czarina Elizabeth of Russia. Her successor, Peter III, was a warm admirer of the Prussian king; he not only deserted the coalition, but sent a Russian detachment to Frederick's support. With the turn of the tide the French court, weary of the struggle, made a separate peace, and Maria Theresa, forsaken by both her allies, was forced to acquiesce a third time in the loss of Silesia. The Treaty of Hubertsburg, concluded in February, 1763, reëstablished the *status quo ante* between Austria and Prussia in every particular.

THE EMPEROR JOSEPH II

YOUTH AND EDUCATION OF JOSEPH, 1741-1765

Born in 1741, the eldest son of Maria Theresa and Francis of Lorraine, Joseph II was still a youth of twenty-two when the Peace of Hubertsburg was signed. His childhood had coincided with one war, the struggle over the question of his mother's succession; and the Seven Years' War (1756-1763), when the attention of Europe was focussed upon the campaigns of Frederick the Great, found him at the most impressionable period of youth. Seized with military enthusiasm, he begged permission to serve with the Austrian forces; but when this ambition was repressed his mood changed to one of apparent apathy.

Two influences in particular shaped the growth of Joseph's ideals: the writings of the *philosophes* and the example of Frederick the Great. All the children of

Maria Theresa were badly educated; Joseph lacked a grounding in the exact sciences and had little appreciation of art or literature. For the problems of statecraft, however, he manifested a lively interest. His most eminent instructor in the science of government was Karl Anton Martini, a disciple of the German philosopher Wolff, and a leader of the Enlightenment in the Austrian lands. Martini's writings indicate that he was a convert to the theory of natural law in its most dogmatic form. That Joseph was influenced by his views and accepted them with favor may be surmised from the honors he later conferred upon his tutor; but it would be a mistake to attribute to any one source ideas which were the property of all enlightened thinkers in that age. Joseph might have found similar doctrines in any work of the *philosophes* which he studied.

JOSEPH AS CO-REGENT, 1765-1780

In Maria Theresa's nature the heart of a woman was joined to the mind and spirit of a king; though not the equal of a Catharine or an Elizabeth, she must be ranked among the great queens of history. A sovereign in her own right, she refused to share her authority; despite the extravagant love she felt for Francis of Lorraine, she early recognized his incompetence, and never allowed him more than a shadow of the imperial dignity. When he died in 1764 Joseph had already been chosen to succeed him as Holy Roman Emperor, but again the title was to carry little power. Though appointed co-regent with his mother, Joseph obtained no share in the management of internal affairs. He was allowed to interest himself in the reorganization of the army, and in foreign politics; but his freedom of action was so carefully circumscribed that on two occasions he begged to resign his dignities unless he could enjoy the measure of authority which should by right pertain to them. The conflict between mother and son became at times so bitter that Maria Theresa spoke of retiring to a nunnery; but in the end, Joseph, who was a dutiful son, always yielded, accepting as gracefully as he could his ineffective rôle.

The secret of his frustration lay as much in his own character as in his mother's opposition. It is the fate of princes to have few real friends, but had Joseph possessed the personality for it he might have headed a party of reform, or forced his way into the government by some other method. Unfortunately his nature was cold and unmagnetic, and he failed to create confidence or attract a following. Though he could assume at will an air of candor and informality, Frederick the Great detected at their first meeting that his frankness was simulated. Nor did Joseph's superficial education escape the sharp judgment of the Prussian king. "With all his desire to acquire knowledge," the latter wrote, "he lacks the patience to teach himself." Yet Frederick did not despise, nor altogether dislike this "Cæsar possessed by demons." Perhaps he recollected the craving for glory and the impatience of restraint which had tormented him in his own youth.

Frederick had been given a chance to gratify his

ambitious nature by conquering Silesia at twenty-nine; but Joseph, as he passed into his thirties and found his schemes as far as ever from realization, developed a stubborn and bitter sense of frustration. No doubt of himself or of his methods troubled him, but he became more and more exasperated with the stupidity of others. Much as he had studied the character of Frederick, that monarch's greatest quality had escaped him. Frederick, as Carlyle has said, was a Reality. He possessed the clarity of vision of a genius; he judged himself with the same cynical realism that he applied to others, and was the first to admit his own failures and mistakes. To Joseph such impersonal analysis was impossible. He was a poor judge of men; he had mediocre talents and the mind of a doctrinaire; his one approach to genius was his infinite capacity for taking pains.

Few rulers have worked more conscientiously. He plagued his mother with unsolicited projects for the abolition of serfdom, the suppression of the monasteries, the proclamation of religious toleration. But Maria Theresa would not disrupt the social order unduly, and Joseph's anti-clerical sentiments shocked her orthodoxy. In her own cautious manner she had introduced many reforms—in education, in agriculture, in finance, and in the Church. The Inquisition was suppressed in Milan; the use of torture was restricted; the Jesuits were expelled from the Hapsburg domains. Such concessions to the spirit of the Enlightenment Joseph regarded as palliative measures, little better than useless so long as the basic principles of government went unreformed.

"The work piles up daily," he wrote his brother Leopold in 1772, "and nothing is done. I labor unceasingly all morning, and until five and six in the afternoon, with fifteen minutes out while I eat a solitary lunch, but there is no result. The petty objections, the intrigues, of which I have so long been the victim, hinder and obstruct me, and with the delay everything is going to the devil."

FIRST PARTITION OF POLAND, 1772

So Joseph turned his attention to foreign affairs. Out of admiration for Frederick he urged an alliance with Prussia, and Maria Theresa was at last persuaded to let him visit that kingdom. In 1769 Catharine of Russia was pressing a victorious campaign against the Turks which filled the Viennese court with alarm; it was hoped that Austria and Prussia, if united, might check the Muscovite ambitions. Joseph met the great enemy of his House at Neisse, and succumbed at once to the fascination of Frederick's personality. "We talked," he wrote his mother, "of legislation, of Voltaire, of a hundred things which it is impossible to recount." A sense of caution, it may be, kept him from being more explicit; he was aware of the disapproval with which Maria Theresa regarded the king of Prussia's unorthodox opinions. "I hear," Voltaire wrote Frederick, "that you have been initiating the Emperor into our holy mysteries."

As a diplomat Joseph proved himself naïve and not very successful. The following year a second interview was arranged between the two monarchs, but this time it was the Austrian minister Kaunitz who negotiated the agreement. War between Austria and Russia over the Turkish question appeared all but unavoidable. Frederick, who had friendly understandings with both states, labored to avert hostilities, and the dispute was finally settled by all three powers agreeing to seek compensation by annexing a portion of Poland. The result was a race between Austrian, Prussian, and Russian troops to occupy coveted sections of that defenceless country; and this First Portion of Poland, as it is termed, was ratified by a treaty signed at St. Petersburg in 1772. The responsibility for this act of unwarranted aggression must be divided among the three courts, but the Austrian participation was perhaps the least excusable.

THE POTATO WAR (1778-1779)

It has already been pointed out how Austria and France, by a readjustment of alliances known as the Diplomatic Revolution, foreswore their ancient rivalry in a compact for mutual defence in 1756. That this agreement outlasted the Seven Years' War must be credited to the endeavours of the Austrian minister Kaunitz, for it was unpopular in both Paris and Vienna. Joseph, in particular, was hostile towards the French Court; and Louis XVI (1774-1793), though he had married the Emperor's sister Marie Antoinette, distrusted and disliked his brother-in-law. Fear of the Russians, however, held Austria from breaking with France, and in 1777 Joseph was despatched to Paris in an attempt to establish the alliance on a firmer foundation. As a diplomatic overture the visit was a failure; it served merely to disgust Joseph with Parisian frivolity, and to convince him more strongly than ever of the worthlessness of the agreement.

The House of Austria derived in truth little real advantage from an alliance with the Bourbons; the Court of Versailles, while collaborating in minor matters, blocked every important Hapsburg ambition; and the Emperor had barely ended his stay in Paris when a crisis taught him unmistakably the hollowness of French friendship. In December, 1777, the Elector of Bavaria died without male issue, and Joseph, imitating Frederick's Silesian *coup*, immediately laid claim to, and occupied, a third of the Bavarian domains. Ever vigilant to resist Hapsburg aggression, Frederick protested vigorously. As the diplomatic argument grew tense both Austria and Prussia despatched large armies into the field; for Joseph, while protesting his desire for peace, burned with secret ambition to try his skill against the greatest general of the age. But Maria Theresa would not support his warlike attitude. Without his knowledge she wrote to Frederick begging him to avert bloodshed, and to Catharine the Great invoking Russian mediation. France, the ally of Austria, renounced her treaty obligations and refused the stipulated aid. Swift to gauge the change in the currents, and finding Joseph's army well intrenched, Frederick preferred to win his point by diplomacy. The campaign from which Joseph had planned to gain renown passed off without a battle, and because of the activity of the troops in hunting forage was ridiculed by contemporaries as the Potato War. By the terms of peace signed at Teschen in May, 1779, Austria was compelled to withdraw from all but a fraction of the disputed territory.

CATHARINE THE GREAT OF RUSSIA (1762-1796)

Maria Theresa's appeal for Russian assistance in settling the Bavarian quarrel was a flattering recognition of the position attained by Russia under the energetic control of Catharine the Great. This German princess, who had dethroned her husband and at thirty-three become sole Autocrat of all the Russias, is commonly ranked as an enlightened despot, but Catharine's enlightenment was largely a pose. In the lonely years of her early married life she had read avidly the works of Voltaire, Montesquieu, and Diderot, preparing herself for the great rôle she meant one day to play in Russian affairs. She professed a deep admiration for the *philosophes,* and corresponded with many of them; and they in turn flattered her with exaggerated praise. In practical affairs, however, Catharine, like Frederick the Great, was a realist, and she did not permit her doctrinaire inclinations to blind her to the fact that she had been called to rule like an oriental despot over a semi-barbarous people.

There is some difference of opinion as to the value

of Catharine's reforms. The deposition and murder of her husband, the Czar Peter III, in 1762, made Catharine mistress of a vast and unwieldy empire, governed through a highly centralized administration. At first she entertained the liberal project of creating a system of provincial estates to be elected by the people and entrusted with the management of local affairs. When the estates were instituted, however, the real authority remained in the hands of a governor appointed from St. Petersburg, and the reform did not affect the improvement in provincial administration which had been anticipated. In a similar fashion Catharine's desire to emancipate and educate the lower classes failed because of the passive resistance of her officials, and her sympathy for the serfs did not prevent an actual increase in serfdom during her reign. Whatever her good intentions, she dared not offend the bureaucracy and the class of privileged land-owners upon whose support she depended to maintain her position. There was a vast discrepancy between Catharine's theories and her practices, a discrepancy perhaps best illustrated by her plan for legal reform. Inspired by the works of the Physiocrats she determined to discover the natural laws upon which the legislation of her empire ought to repose and reconstruct the civil code accordingly. In 1767 she wrote an "Instruction to the Commission appointed to prepare a draft for a new code," and called an assembly to carry out the project. It soon became evident that the task was a more difficult one than had been supposed; the discussions of the Commission dragged interminably; it ceased to meet regularly, finally ceased to meet at all; and the whole project was forgotten. This failure, and the failure of Catharine's other reforms, serves to indicate the weakness of enlightened despotism as a mode of government. Though she possessed unusual gifts and enjoyed presumedly autocratic powers, Catharine could not overcome singlehanded the resistance of the privileged orders, nor rouse from their apathy the millions of serfs resigned fatalistically to their lot.

A greater degree of success attended Catharine's foreign policies. Though born a German, she managed to acquire an intimate knowledge of the interests of her adopted country. It was her ambition to see the Russian Empire play a part in European affairs commensurate with its resources; and this ambition was strengthened by the annexation of Polish territory in 1772 which gave Russia a pretext for interfering in the Germanies. In the south Catharine pressed a war against the Turks with such success that she had dreams of reëstablishing the defunct Byzantine Empire at Constantinople. Frederick the Great, who "feared the Russians more than God," paid Catharine a yearly subsidy; Maria Theresa flattered her by soliciting her intervention, as a sort of arbiter of Europe, in the Potato War. Catharine's foreign policy had attained the measure of success which its consistency deserved.

Between the Courts of Vienna and St. Petersburg the shadow of the Turkish question had long excited a mutual mistrust; but in 1780 Joseph decided that it was best to agree with this Muscovite adversary quickly.

For the reverse which Austria had suffered in the Potato War he held French perfidy to blame; but he dared not break with his Bourbon ally while Russia remained unfriendly. Taking advantage of Catharine's notorious love of flattery, he requested permission to visit Russia in the rôle of Count Falkenstein, travelling without retinue or ceremony, and solely for the purpose of meeting Her Imperial Majesty. Catharine "found it impossible to disguise the joy which his letter brought her"; and Joseph, in the course of a visit which lasted several weeks, had the satisfaction of dispelling the spirit of unfriendliness between Austria and Russia, and of weakening Prussian influence at the Court of St. Petersburg. But the price of the understanding, inevitably, was to be Austrian assistance for Catharine's Turkish policy. Joseph's air of frankness had proved no match for Catharine's feline duplicity, and the old fable of the chestnuts and the fire was to be reënacted, with the rôles reversed.

JOSEPH AS SOLE RULER, 1780-1790

To the end of her forty year reign Maria Theresa held the affairs of government in a firm hand; but her death in 1780 bequeathed to Joseph the undivided sovereignty of the empire. The new ruler was in his fortieth year, imperious and self-willed, impatient of restraints upon his authority and unscrupulous in the use of it. Existing portraits of him show a face handsome and animated; he had the long nose of the Hapsburgs and eyes of the purest blue; but the frankness of his gaze was belied by the tightly pursed lips, and his forehead though lofty was over-narrow.

Behind Joseph's zeal for reform lay a humanitarian concern for the happiness of his subjects. Governments existed, it seemed clear to him, in order that they might safeguard the welfare of the people. His political researches had convinced him that the most efficient form of government was a highly organized machine which could absorb into a central bureaucracy the details of local administration, and establish throughout the realm a rigid uniformity of language, law, and custom. To introduce simplicity and standardization into the chaotic administration of the Hapsburg dominions appeared to him the evident duty of an enlightened despot; but behind this humanistic zeal lay an unacknowledged motive, a desire to make himself master of an aggressive, centralized, military state.

FINANCIAL REFORMS

Physiocratic doctrines had exercised too strong a sway over Joseph's thinking for him to doubt that sound finances were the bases of efficient government. As co-regent he had labored to balance the Austrian budget, subscribing part of his personal fortune to achieve the desired result; but at his accession an accurate estimate of the revenue and expenditure of the state was still unobtainable. The problem of accumulating capital, of enriching himself and his people, claimed his closest attention. He lived simply, almost frugally, indifferent to the charges of miserliness which his economies brought him. "Saving and scrimping," jeered Frederick, "saving and scrimping, that is all he sets his heart upon."

The Emperor's passion for fiscal experiments excited little enthusiasm among his subjects: parsimony is an unprincely virtue. Furthermore, his attempts to make each taxpayer a direct contributor to the royal exchequer struck too definitely at the feudal system to escape bitter opposition; and the scheme for protective tariffs which he introduced pleased only a few manufacturers. "In financial matters," he wrote Leopold of Tuscany, "I can not find a soul who understands me or has a single idea of the elements of the thing. In all honor, I do not know how I am going to manage."

Yet he held himself stubbornly to the task until the years of soul-devouring toil had their reward. In 1786 the Austrian budget showed a revenue of eighty-eight million gulden against an expenditure of eighty-five million. It was a fleeting triumph. The following year witnessed the outbreak of a ruinous war with Turkey, and Joseph's last months were clouded by the knowledge that despite all his expedients he must leave to his successor a national debt which extended at the time of his death to four hundred million gulden.

RELIGIOUS REFORMS

As a child of the Enlightenment, Joseph favored a wide tolerance in religious affairs. He was no free-thinker; to the end of his life he remained a circum-

spect if not an ardent communicant of the Roman
Catholic Church; but like Frederick the Great he felt
that his subjects might safely be left to seek the road
to heaven after their own fashion. One of the first
edicts which followed his accession proclaimed the
equality of non-Catholics before the law. Permission was accorded members of the heretical sects to
hold civil or military office, to erect churches of their
own, to establish schools and seminaries. Even the
Jews were allowed to lay aside the peculiar costume
which had been for centuries the symbol of their
humiliating status.

As a further step Joseph decided to disestablish the
monasteries. Their wealth was a source of annoyance
to him; it irked his economic soul that gold should lie
idle when it might be circulating to the common good.
He disliked moreover to have in his dominions brotherhoods, the members of which stood outside the jurisdiction of the civil courts, and looked to Rome for their
instructions. Successive decrees limited the number of
monks and nuns that might be admitted to the cloister;
a pension was provided for members of the disestab-
lished orders; and monks so desiring were encouraged
to take up secular occupations. Leopold of Tuscany
observed with interest the progress of these hardy
measures, but he declined to keep pace with them.
"In Italy," he explained to Joseph, "the people are
much more deeply attached to the brotherhoods than
in Germany." Perhaps, with the tact characteristic of
him, he wished to sound a note of caution, but if so the
warning passed unheeded.

Even the ritual of the Church did not escape Joseph's attention. A contempt for ceremonial display was one of his strongest characteristics, and this, combined with the impatience of the rationalist at a complicated liturgy, led him to attempt a simplification of the Church services. For the money commonly lavished upon gilded images and superfluous pageantry he found more practical uses, and the same desire for economy moved him to forbid all processions and pilgrimages. At the same time fifteen Saints' Days were stricken from the calendar on the ground that they afforded the people too many holidays. Work was more important than worship.

Papal protests at this rough treatment of the Church proving of no avail, Pope Pius VI decided in 1782 to visit Vienna in person. Unable to dissuade the Holy Father from his purpose, Joseph prepared to welcome him with every show of respect; but he refused to moderate his anti-clerical measures in any particular. The rationalists of Europe enjoyed the spectacle of papal impotence and affected to marvel at the courtesy and forebearance with which Joseph treated his uninvited guest. "I do not envy Your Majesty the rare privilege of being lodged face to face with Pius VI," wrote Catharine. ". . . A priest like that is a somewhat incommodious piece of furniture." Joseph's reply echoed the same note of irreverence. "The interest, may I venture to say the friendliness, with which Her Majesty has written regarding the Italian priest who recently oppressed me with his visit warms me with gratitude. . . . The Pope gained nothing of importance; but I managed to treat him in such a manner as to avoid a definite rupture."

The program pursued by Joseph in ecclesiastical matters, which in its ultimate implications aimed at the complete subordination of the church to the state and the severance of all effective bonds with Rome, antic-ipated many of the developments of the French Revo-lution and of the nineteenth century. Like the leaders of the Revolution he planned to confiscate all church lands, and to make the priesthood dependent upon a state salary. The action of the Italian kingdom in more recent times, and of the Third French Republic, in dissolving all ties between state and church, is an outgrowth of the policy known as "Josephism."

JURISTIC REFORMS

Of the confusion which distinguished the administra-tion of justice under the old régime, the overlapping jurisdictions, the conflicting codes, the arbitrary ar-rests and inhuman punishments, no adequate picture can be attempted here. Within the confines of a single province the same offence might involve penalties which ranged from a light fine to mutilation or death; yet as the *philosophes* never tired of pointing out, it was im-possible that there could be two punishments for the same crime and both of them just. The voice of reason and of humanity urged the suppression of the many courts and codes, and the establishment in their place of a uniform system of civil and criminal law applicable in every instance.

In the Austrian lands justice was confused by a mass of customs, charters, feudal privileges, papal proclamations, and imperial edicts, which formed a legal tangle past all unravelling. Maria Theresa appointed a commission of lawyers in 1753 to codify the existing legislation; after fourteen years it published eight volumes of decrees, but the work was less a code than a collection. A compilation of the criminal laws, the *Nemesis Theresiana,* was published in 1768; but this likewise bore that stamp of incompleteness which impaired the value of almost all Maria Theresa's reforms.

As Joseph envisaged it the administration of justice was a simple function of the state, his idea of legal reform being to solve all disputes by establishing throughout the Empire the single jurisdiction of the imperial courts. A supreme council at Vienna, appellate courts in the larger cities, and magistracies for each town, were the elements of his plan; but since he could not shatter to bits the sorry scheme of things as he found it, the problem of remolding it proved beyond his skill. Concessions and compromises soon blotted the bold outlines of his project; thick-headed subordinates completed the confusion. His new codes pleased no one: jurists in the Netherlands fought the abolition of torture; humanists in Vienna condemned the new scale of punishments as merciless; the privileged classes everywhere stood aghast at a decree which established civil equality before the law. In the presence of a universal and insistent clamor of disapproval Joseph hardened his heart.

ADMINISTRATIVE REFORMS

Familiar from his youth with the exercise of military authority, the new Emperor had carried into the affairs of civil administration an inflexibility of temper reminiscent of barrack-room discipline. An empire, he felt, like an army, required a centralized command; he would have agreed with Dupont de Nemours that the idea of several authorities in the same state was an absurdity. The triumph of his ideals required the destruction of the feudal courts, of the provincial estates, the monastic orders, in fact of all autonomous groups in the empire, and the substitution of an imperial bureaucracy in which the Church, the army, the judiciary, were each to be a department of government officered by civil servants.

A beginning had been made in this direction by the creation of a Council of State at Vienna in 1761. By appointing a hierarchy of royal officials, and shifting to them the authority previously vested in the nobles, the national monarchs of Europe had found a way to humble their feudal dependents. It was a policy which Louis XIV of France had pursued with particular success, and Joseph planned to follow it unswervingly in the Hapsburg lands. When the suppression of the provincial estates and the curtailment of local liberties alarmed his Belgian and Hungarian subjects and finally goaded them into revolution he was at a loss to understand their opposition to measures so clearly salutary. "I leave you to judge the extent of my despair," he wrote Leopold. "I am the only one holding to the true course, and I am left to labor it alone. The Council of State avails as little as if it had never existed. I am without any assistance whatsoever. Despatches, replies, everything is left for me to attend to." Joseph was reaping the difficulties of solitary despotism.

EDUCATIONAL REFORMS

All the leaders of the Enlightenment attached great importance to the problem of education; a child rationally reared, it seemed to them, could not fail to become an intelligent and virtuous citizen. Public instruction had been neglected in the past; but it was too important a function to be resigned indefinitely to village schoolmasters, or left in the hands of the Church. In this field, as in all others, Joseph entertained enlightened but dogmatic views. He proposed to amalgamate the Austrian universities, together with the intermediate and primary schools, into a single system, and to administer them as a department of government. A revised curriculum and state-salaried teachers were to grind out a steady stream of efficient civil servants; the schools would become factories, machines for making more machines.

Nor would maturity bring to the citizens an escape from state tutelage. Frederick the Great once boasted that he and his subjects had an unofficial bargain: he was to do as he liked and they might say what they pleased; but the Austrian peoples under Joseph II could pretend to no such privilege. A paternal government treated them as children, and their manners and morals were made the object of a constant and irritating supervision. Before it came into their hands, all reading matter had to pass a board of censorship; foreign periodicals were excluded from the Hapsburg dominions; and large rewards were posted for the apprehension of unauthorized pamphleteers. Petitions on behalf of freedom of speech or of the press left Joseph unmoved. "The father of a family," he said, "who holds the welfare of his children at heart must not allow himself to be turned from a salutary course because of ill-judged complaints."

SOCIAL REFORMS

Since of all classes in the state the serfs alone had nothing to lose they could afford to view without alarm the headstrong course of the reforming emperor. Indeed, long after his death stories of his simplicity, his accessibility, his democratic tastes, were preserved among the peasants whose welfare he had striven to promote. For the noble orders Joseph had little use; to a distrust born of political exigencies he added a dislike that was purely personal; and his humane decrees for the liberation of the serfs neglected to provide adequate compensation for the masters. Hence, not unnaturally, the nobles showed no noticeable enthusiasm for the success of the emperor's measures: the liberated serfs were left to shift for themselves; most of them proved unequal to the responsibilities of their new estate; and some were reduced to eating the bark of trees to avoid starvation. The blame for these misfortunes the emperor, as always, attributed to the malice and stupidity of others. "I lack servants of every sort," he complained, "either for planning or for executing my designs. To be frank, I have found scarcely one person who is filled with a genuine zeal for the good of the country."

Joseph never learned to suffer fools gladly. "The emperor," laments the diary of a councillor, "acts as if . . . he alone loved the country and knew what was right, and all his subordinates were either rascals or blockheads." The letters to Leopold of Tuscany tell the same story. "No one here has assimilated the rules I laid down," concludes one exasperated passage. "The heads of the civil service still follow their old ruts, signing without a glance at the contents any paper that is set before them." And again, "This business of repeating the same thing week after week is killing me." Yet even in his blackest moods a sense of duty held him to his task. "I have been slaving away in my study," he confesses in one place, "seeking some means to organize and simplify my work a little; but laboring against so many obstacles has reduced me to such a pitch of hopelessness that were my heart not set upon the thing I would have to give up in despair."

The Foreign Policies of Joseph II

THE RE-OPENING OF THE SCHELDT

By the Peace of Westphalia (1648) which ended the Thirty Years' War the river Scheldt was closed to all save Dutch ships, and a line of barrier fortresses erected in the Spanish Netherlands to protect the frontier between France and Holland. When the Spanish Netherlands passed to the House of Austria by the Treaty of Utrecht (1713) these terms remained in force; for by closing the Scheldt the merchants of Amsterdam had been able to cut off the sea-trade of Antwerp, and to profit by their rival's decline.

Joseph II began his reign with the intention already formed of abolishing this restriction upon the trade of his Belgian provinces. In 1782, finding Holland at war with Great Britain, he seized the opportunity to repudiate the convention closing the Scheldt, at the same time dismantling the barrier fortresses in an endeavor to conciliate France. As usual his calculations miscarried. The first ship which he despatched to Antwerp was fired upon by the Dutch; French assistance, upon which he had built high hopes, failed to materialize; Russia was secretly hostile. Baffled, Joseph consented after long quibbling to renounce his project; but to cover his defeat he demanded from the Dutch an indemnity of ten million gulden. Relieved to see the matter settled, the powers assisted him to collect it. *Trinkgeld* (a tip) was Frederick's contemptuous epithet for the transaction.

THE BAVARIAN QUESTION AGAIN

The ill-success which thus attended his aggressive policy in the Low Countries may have helped to turn Joseph's mind back to another project of his, the exchange of his Belgian provinces for Bavaria. By the Peace of Teschen, which closed the Potato War in 1779, the House of Austria had renounced all further claims upon the electorate, but even if Joseph had possessed a tender conscience about such promises (which was far from being the case) the thought of rounding out his empire by the addition of a wealthy dukedom might well have subdued his scruples. Lying between Bohemia and the Rhine, Bavaria seemed naturally fitted to become a corner-stone of the Austrian Empire, and to assure for all time the predominance of the Hapsburgs in German affairs.

To Charles Theodore, the reigning elector, Joseph offered in 1784 the title of King of Burgundy, with Brussels for his capital, if he would hand over Bavaria to the Imperial Crown. Few transactions, even in that age of cynical diplomacy, showed a more complete disregard for the wishes of the subject peoples; Bavaria and the Austrian Netherlands were to be bought and sold like country estates. For the House of Austria the exchange promised striking advantages; the Belgian provinces were alien and inaccessible, while Bavaria, with a population of nearly three million German Catholics, could be assimilated into the empire and would protect the northern frontier. Joseph pressed on the negotiations with zeal.

From his retreat at *Sans Souci* the aging Frederick watched the plot mature. Charles Theodore, it was evident, had sold himself to Austria; but his heir, the Duke of Zweibrücken, had still to be consulted, and might be persuaded, by judicious hints, to oppose the Hapsburg schemes. In January, 1785, the emperor's projects met with sudden disaster. The Duke of Zweibrücken protested against the negotiations and appealed to Frederick for justice; and the people of Bavaria, learning with indignation of the fate proposed for them, so frightened Charles Theodore that he denied all knowledge of the proposed exchange. At *Sans Souci* Frederick accepted the compliments of ambassadors on his unselfish solicitude for the rights of the Bavarians. He suggested the formation of a league of German princes to put a stop to Joseph's aggressions. It amused the conqueror of Silesia to pose as a champion of order and legitimacy.

THE ROAD TO BYZANTIUM

The alliance between Austria and Russia born of Joseph's visit to St. Petersburg in 1780 had as its object the aggrandizement of both powers at the expense of Turkey. How the spoils of conquest were to be divided had been left for the moment unsettled; but both Joseph and Catharine had visions of entering Constantinople in triumph and reviving the ancient glories of Byzantium. Their alliance was thus an unnatural one, and any success won by either power was certain to strain their friendly understanding. In the nineteenth century the continued decline of Turkey sharpened the eagerness of both Austria and Russia to outwit the other in winning the Turkish heritage, and their intrigues created the problem known in diplomatic history as "The Near Eastern Question."

Until it fell into the hands of the Turks in 1453, Constantinople had been the capital of the Eastern Roman Empire. As successor of Charlemagne Joseph dreamed of making it once again acknowledge the sway of an Emperor Ever August of the Romans. In December, 1787, partly in the hope of taking the Turks by surprise, partly to anticipate Catharine, he launched an army of 200,000 men against Belgrade. This discreditable manœuver (there had been no declaration of war) failed in its objective; the campaign of 1788 turned against the Austrians, and Joseph's army, attacked on the flank, was forced into a disastrous retreat. Catharine made no real effort to relieve her ally; she had intended from the first to let Joseph draw upon himself the malignance of the Turks and the disapproval of Europe. Protected from invasion herself by the wide Russian steppes, she watched the Austrian cordons writhe and struggle in their vain efforts to save the smiling valleys of the Banat from the fury of the Ottoman hordes.

The morbid mind of the emperor led him to exaggerate a reverse into a catastrophe; in desperation he cashiered general after general as responsible for a disaster which he had himself invited. "Nothing more terrible, more piteous, more shameful, could have happened," he wrote Leopold. "My plans have all been destroyed by those who should have forwarded them. I demand of you whether I am not the most wretched being alive, enduring the utmost that it is possible to bear of moral and physical suffering?" Mental distress, added to the hardships of the campaign, had broken his health; but unable to accept the fact of his own incompetence he refused to resign the command of the army. "I would rather die under a tree," he protested, "than abandon things in their present state, for the Marshall is so discouraged himself that he no longer knows what to do." He held out until December, when the troops had somewhat recovered their morale. Then, so weak that he could scarcely ride a horse, he returned to Vienna.

THE LAST PHASE

The program of internal reforms, entrusted to subordinates during the emperor's absence in the field, had become involved in a more hopeless confusion than ever. With the concentration of troops in the south the Austrian Netherlands were left free to assert their independence, an opportunity of which they had taken prompt advantage. This revolt of Joseph's Belgian subjects is exceptional enough to deserve notice, for it was inspired not by a desire for reforms but by opposition to them. The emperor's cancellation of established privileges and his substitution of nine governors and a central council in place of the complex institutions under which the provinces had been ruled since the Middle Ages angered the Belgians to the point of revolution. The hatred of Austria thus fostered led them two years later to welcome the French revolutionary armies, and to accept willingly in the name of liberty reforms more drastic than those Joseph had introduced in the name of efficiency. Few examples could illustrate better the hatred which Joseph was capable of inspiring, or prove more clearly the innate weakness of enlightened despotism as a method of reform.

The Belgian revolution was not the only problem that faced Joseph when he returned to Vienna at the close of 1788. A revolt was likewise threatening among the natives of the Tyrol; and the nobles of Hungary were on the point of throwing off their allegiance to the House of Hapsburg. With that close application which had become a habit with him the emperor sought to study the causes of the general discontent. He studied despatches, questioned officials, and called for the minutes of the various councils. But his old power of concentration had gone; the slightest effort or excitement set his pulse racing; his head ached interminably.

Thoughts of the work that was piling up pursued him, crowding all relaxation from his days and filling the nights with disquietude. Ten years of failure had passed since he talked so confidently of reform with Frederick at Neisse, and the Prussian king warned him against that slavery to details which is a vexation to the spirit and blinds it to the larger things of life. Now Frederick was dead and Joseph was dying. "I am distressed that your cough should prove so persistent," Leopold had written more than once. In April, 1789, came the first hemorrhage. "The ailment which has been tormenting me these nine months," he wrote Leopold, "suddenly resulted in a vomiting of blood. . . . They applied leeches, but I still continued to cough up blood, more in fact than ever. . . ." Leeches for a pulmonary hemorrhage!

His last months Joseph passed in solitude, almost unattended. "I am unable to leave my room," he wrote in December. "I receive no one, for it is difficult to sustain a conversation, and I am left alone with my problems and my thoughts which are not happy ones." Kaunitz refused outright to visit the emperor's sick-room; lesser functionaries became evasive or unmanageable. Slowly the conviction established itself in Joseph's mind that his officials either would not or could not execute his commands, and the consciousness of failure obsessed him. "Here lies Joseph II," ran his self-chosen epitaph, "who was unfortunate in everything that he undertook." On January 30, 1790, he withdrew all his reforms; the task of tranquillizing the distracted empire was his bequest to the more tactful Leopold. He died the 20th of February, a man, in the words of Lord Bryce, "than whom few have more narrowly missed greatness."

CHAPTER III

SOME LESSER DESPOTS

THE EMPEROR LEOPOLD II

As Joseph II left no children, the Hapsburg lands passed at his death to his brother Leopold, the same Leopold of Tuscany to whom he had so frequently written concerning his hopes and his anxieties. Leopold shared all Joseph's eagerness for reform but he united with it a conciliatory spirit and a talent for diplomacy. A long apprenticeship as ruler of a small principality (he became Grand Duke of Tuscany at the age of nineteen) taught him the difficulties of administrative reconstruction. In 1765, together with his young wife Marie Louise, daughter of Charles III of Spain, he took up his residence in Florence. Maria Theresa, who was always hesitant about trusting her children with authority, kept him in tutelage for five years, but after 1770 he was permitted to introduce some of the reforms which he had meditated. His enthusiasm and energy infused a new spirit into the lethargic administration of his Tuscan duchy.

Leopold's legislative program contained little that was original, nor did it need to do so. The experiments of other enlightened princes and the essays of the *philosophes* left no shortage of either precepts or examples by which he might profit. Improvements in the fiscal system enabled him to reduce taxation yet increase the revenue. Roads were built, marshes drained, new crops introduced; restrictions on trade and commerce disappeared and agriculture flourished. The wisdom of Leopold's measures rendered Tuscany one of the happiest and most prosperous of the Italian states, and earned for its ruler the flattery of the *philosophes*. Mirabeau was proud to claim him as a royal convert to physiocracy—"A convinced and unswerving disciple of the science"—and Leopold in return recognized *L'ami des hommes* as the head of the physiocratic school.

More praiseworthy even than his zeal for administrative efficiency was Leopold's activity on behalf of the most wretched class of his subjects, the criminals. Humanitarianism was a virtue much affected by the *philosophes;* they loved to pose as the champions of the oppressed, and would burst into facile tears at a tale of cruelty or injustice. Nor was their emotion altogether insincere. The brutal and stupid criminal codes of the day filled them with disgust and apprehension, and won their sympathy for the victims of the law. Eighteenth century justice provided spectacles calculated to move the most indifferent onlooker to pity, for the cruel and unusual punishments inflicted— branding, mutilation, breaking on the wheel, hanging, drawing and quartering—were often carried out in public. The barbarity of the punishments, the arbitrary and unequal manner in which they were enforced, and the disproportion between the offences and the penalties, could hardly fail to compel the attention of thoughtful men.

Of the protests called forth by these pitiless practices the most influential was *An Essay on Crimes and
Punishments* published by the Marquis Beccaria in
1764. In the name of reason and of humanity Beccaria
appealed to society to alter its attitude towards the
problem of crime and its repression. The purpose of
the law, he urged, should not be so much the punishment of crimes as their prevention. The right of self-
protection society might justly claim, the right of revenge never. This humane reasoning was destined in
time to change the whole philosophy of criminal juris-
prudence. "The end of punishment," Beccaria wrote,
"is no other than to prevent the criminal doing further injury to society, and to prevent others from com-
mitting the like offence." The belief that society must
exact retribution on every offender against the law,
even though the offence had injured nobody, he proclaimed absurd; and the spectacle of an occasional victim dragged to public execution, far, he asserted, from
serving as a salutary warning, tended rather to bru-
talize and degrade the masses.

Torture as a method of forcing confessions likewise
drew from Beccaria a reasoned denunciation. It was
illogical, he pointed out, that the same man should be
both accuser and accused, and evidence extracted under torture had been shown again and again to be un-
reliable. Furthermore, if the court possessed evidence
sufficient to convict a man without his own confession,
to extract a confession by torture was superfluous; if
the court did not possess the evidence to convict the
accused, then they would be torturing an innocent man.

For, "No man can be judged a criminal until he be found guilty. . . . If he be not guilty, you torture the innocent, for in the eye of the law everyone is innocent whose crime has not been proved."

The most daring of Beccaria's recommendations, and the one which excited the loudest opposition, was his plea for the abolition of the death penalty. Public executions, with all their barbaric accompaniments of torture and mutilation, were less effective, he insisted, than lighter sentences firmly and swiftly imposed. The laws of the state should be like the laws of nature: in nature there were neither rewards nor punishments, there were only consequences; yet all rational men obeyed the laws of nature because they knew them to be universal and implacable. If criminals were convinced that a penalty, even a moderate penalty, must prove the swift and inevitable consequence of every crime, they would seldom commit an unlawful, act. For as Beccaria clearly observed, "Crimes are more effectually prevented by the *certainty* than the *severity* of the punishment."

Fearing the enmity of the unenlightened, Beccaria had published his treatise anonymously, but he found support and encouragement from the Hapsburg princes who ruled in his native Italy. Leopold adopted many of his views in reforming the penal code of Tuscany; he forbade the use of torture and abolished the death penalty save in cases of parricide or *lèse-majesté*. In Austrian Lombardy, under Leopold's brother, the Archduke Franz, the enlightened Minister, Count Firmian, protected Beccaria from the attacks of his enemies, and in 1768 honored him with an appointment to a chair of political philosophy at Milan.

One form of injustice, which was the most desperate and inexcusable of the age, Beccaria did not venture to attack. "The reader will perceive," he wrote towards the close of his book, "that I have omitted to discuss one class of crimes which has drenched Europe with human blood, and raised up those horrible piles, where strangled cries from amid the black smoke, the crackling of human bones, and the sizzling of still palpitating bowels, provide a pleasant spectacle and sweet music for the fanatical multitude. But men of understanding will appreciate that the age and the country in which I live do not permit me to inquire into the nature of this crime." Beccaria's caution was not unwarranted. The Holy Inquisition had been shorn of a great deal of its power, but it could still occasionally send a man to the stake, even in the eighteenth century. Twenty years after Beccaria wrote, Leopold had the courage, despite the opposition of the Church, to abolish it in the duchy of Tuscany.

Praise must be accorded Leopold for the care and discretion with which he carried through his Tuscan reforms: the Marquis de Mirabeau paid tribute at the time to the "admirable prudence and infinite precautions" with which he acted. His removal to Vienna, on Joseph's death in 1790, might well have been expected to widen his sphere of activity and further the cause of enlightenment, but circumstances forced Leopold, during his short reign of two years, almost into the rôle of a reactionary. Joseph, on his deathbed, had withdrawn his unpopular innovations, and Leopold permitted the reëstablishment of the old institutions in an effort to tranquillize the state. By a policy of mingled conciliation and firmness he was able to pacify the Hungarians, subdue the Netherlands, and conclude an honorable peace with the Turks. His sudden death in 1792 was a misfortune for the Hapsburg lands, for it occurred at a moment when the progress of the French Revolution had rendered the international situation peculiarly difficult to control, and it left the destinies of the Austrian peoples in the incapable hands of Leopold's son and heir, the Emperor Francis II. There were no further reforms; Joseph's efforts appear to have inoculated his subjects against liberal ideas, and Austria was destined to become within a quarter of a century the most reactionary of the great powers.

CHARLES III OF SPAIN

Like Leopold II, Charles III of Spain (1759-1788) was trained for his royal office by an apprenticeship in Italy. The untiring intrigues of his mother, Elizabeth Farnese,[1] secured for him the throne of Naples and Sicily in 1734, and for twenty-five years he strove to promote in that backward and priest-ridden state the principles of enlightened government. Charles was himself a devout Catholic; but clerical opposition to his

---

[1] Elizabeth Farnese, a native of Parma, was the second wife of Philip V of Spain. (1700-1746). Since her son Charles appeared to have little chance of succeeding to the Spanish throne she was determined to win for him a kingdom in her native Italy.

reforms made him an enemy of the Church. With the aid of his energetic Minister Tanucci, he labored perseveringly to reduce the power of the priesthood and to increase the prosperity of his subjects.

Called to the Spanish throne in 1759 by the death of his half-brother Ferdinand, Charles transferred his attention to the mightier task of arresting Spain's decline and turning that country from the path of decadence to which the blind policies of earlier monarchs had committed her. Stirred by stories of his benevolence the Spanish people prepared to welcome him with loyal enthusiasm, but his appearance must have disappointed them a little. Short and round-shouldered, with dark skin, small eyes, and a toothless mouth, he looked more like a broken-down clerk than a king. Court functions and military reviews interested him little. He dressed shabbily, and hated ceremonies. At heart he was an administrator, a king of the new type, honest, conscientious, and deeply absorbed in his responsibilities. In his desire to remodel outworn institutions and to promote the welfare of his people by wise legislation he was a true prince of the Enlightenment; in his jealous retention of authority and his impatience at opposition he was a true despot.

The turbulent conditions in his capital called forth some of Charles' first efforts at reform. Madrid had all the pageantry and picturesqueness, the color and the squalor, of a medieval city. Many of the streets were narrow, dirty, and unsanitary. Badly lighted at night, without police protection, they often proved dangerous to wayfarers, for murder and robbery were common occurrences. In this favorable atmosphere private feuds flourished, for an assailant, wrapped in the anonymous security of a Spanish cloak and sombrero, could achieve his revenge and escape unrecognized, leaving the footpads to shoulder the blame for another deed of violence. In an attempt to remedy this state of affairs Charles ordered the streets cleaned and lighted, organized a police force, and forbade the wearing of long cloaks and broad-brimmed hats. But this last order, crowning as it did a series of reforms which the Spaniards regarded as foreign innovations, stirred the people of Madrid to riot and bloodshed. Frightened by the hostile demonstrations Charles fled from the capital; the unpopular edict was withdrawn, and Squillaci, the minister responsible for its enforcement, was exiled in disgrace.

These Madrid riots of 1766 are of importance chiefly because they provided the anti-Jesuit party at the Court with an argument against the Society of Jesus cogent enough to discredit the latter with the king. The followers of Loyola had long been under suspicion because of their interference in political affairs. Their intrigues had led to their expulsion from Portugal in 1759 and from France in 1764. Charles, however, like the majority of his subjects, was a devout Catholic, and it was necessary to convince him that the Society of Jesus menaced his authority and his life before he could be persuaded to condemn it. The enemies of the Jesuits—members of rival orders like the Augustinians and Franciscans, *philosophes* and Masons, of whom the Count of Aranda was the leader

—seized the opportunity to persuade the king that a Jesuit conspiracy was responsible for the rioting in his capital and that a plot existed to overturn his throne. That Charles accepted the evidence, such as it was, in good faith there seems little reason to doubt. In 1767 he entrusted Aranda with the task of expelling the Jesuits from Spain; the decree was carried out with a secrecy and a suddenness which left the victims no chance to resist. Among the papers seized, it is hardly necessary to add, evidence was soon discovered to prove that a plot to assassinate the king and all the royal family had been frustrated at the eleventh hour.

Frederick the Great, watching with shrewd eyes from the other side of Europe the fate of the Spanish Jesuits, saw more clearly than Charles the truth of the affair. He would not, he observed, go to the trouble of expelling the Jesuits from his dominions; he had need of good school teachers, and he did not suspect them of regicidal intentions. From Rome Pope Clement XIII besought the Spanish king to avoid an over-hasty judgment. "I implore Your Majesty," he wrote, "by the sweet name of Jesus, glorious emblem of the followers of Ignatius; by the name of the Holy Virgin whose immaculate conception they have always defended; by our own advanced years we beg you to relax so great a severity, and to revoke or at least to adjourn your decree until the reasons for it can be discussed with calmness and reflection." But Charles was unshaken. "The motives and the considerations which have driven me to take the resolution referred to, Most Holy Father," he wrote, "are too powerful and too convincing for me to consent to anything less than the expulsion from my realms of the entire Order."

The Jesuits had indeed fallen upon evil days. At the election of a new Pope in 1769, their enemies sought to secure from the successful candidate a promise to suppress the Order entirely. Whether Clement XIV actually committed himself before election seems doubtful; but in 1773 the impatiently awaited bull was finally issued. Out of deference to the wishes of "our very dear sons, the kings of France, Spain, Portugal, and Sicily," the Pope declared the Jesuits deprived of all powers, privileges, and possessions, and the Order itself dissolved and extinguished forever.[1]

Despite his firmness in crushing the Jesuits Charles wavered in his attack upon that other bulwark of the Catholic Church in Spain, the Holy Inquisition. Though he curtailed its powers and declared royal officials immune from its decrees he could not prevent the burning of an occasional mystic or the persecution of free-thinkers. The case of Don Pablo Olavide indicates how dangerous it might prove to earn the displeasure of the Holy Office. The career of Olavide as that of a champion of the Enlightenment in eighteenth century Spain is worth reciting here, not because he was a figure of any great importance, but because, like a cork adrift on the intellectual currents of the time, he marks the ebb and flow of the tide of

[1] The Jesuit Order was reincorporated by a papal edict in 1814 but it has never regained its earlier influence.

rationalism, and its conflict with the forces of orthodoxy.

When Charles III ascended the throne his permission was sought by a group of intellectuals, led by the
Count of Aranda, for a plan to establish agricultural
colonies in the unpeopled wastes of the Sierra Morena
hills. The plan called for the creation of model vil-
lages in which communities were to be established such
as the Physiocrats loved to describe, communities in
which there would be no priests, monks, or other sup-
posedly idle and troublesome persons, but only simple
and industrious citizens who would till the land happily
together under a constitution based upon the laws of
nature. It is at this point that Don Pablo enters the
picture. As a friend of Voltaire and Rousseau, well
and in some quarters unfavorably known for his rationalist views, he was chosen to supervise the colonial venture. The high expectations fostered by the founders
of the settlements were not realized and in 1770 Don
Pablo begged leave to resign his responsibilities. Unorthodox utterances and a thinly veiled contempt for the
priesthood had brought him into disrepute and in 1776
came a summons from the Inquisition. The list of
charges against him included the reading of prohibited
books, listening to the Mass without due respect, possessing indecent pictures and statues, and correspond-
ing with Voltaire. The sentence of the Holy Office
was eight years' imprisonment with confiscation of all
property; but in 1780 Olavide was fortunate in making
his escape to France, where the *philosophes* acclaimed

him as a victim of priestly persecution. The epilogue
to his story shows him in a different light. As a resi-
dent in France Olavide witnessed and applauded the
outbreak of the Revolution; but as he watched the
principles of his philosophy being translated into action he suffered a change of heart. In 1797 he returned to Spain and published his final testament,
*The Gospel Triumphant, or The Conversion of a
Philosopher.*

POMBAL IN PORTUGAL

If the Portuguese kingdom enjoyed a period of enlightened despotism in the second half of the eighteenth
century the credit belongs less to Joseph I (1750-1777)
than to his able but tyrannical minister, Sebastian
Joseph Cavalho, Marquis of Pombal. Under the
direction of this vigorous statesman the whole internal
administration of Portugal was revolutionized. From
1755, the year of the great Lisbon earthquake, when
Pombal's presence of mind in the face of the disaster
earned him the complete confidence of his king, until
the latter's death in 1777, Pombal remained the virtual
dictator of Portugal. Under his direction the finances
were balanced, the legal machinery simplified, and the
educational system improved. In his desire to see
Portugal recover something of her waning greatness he
reorganized the army and attempted to build up a
stronger connection with the Portuguese colonies, a
project which he sought to further by the establishment
of commercial companies with special privileges. The
Jesuits, already engaged in the colonial trade, resented

his interference, and fostered opposition to his plans both in Portugal and America, a policy which hastened the general disaster so soon to overtake their order.

The fame which Pombal won by his energetic reforms, and his patriotic endeavors to liberate Portugal from foreign influences, has been clouded over by the stories of his unbridled despotism. For those who ventured to oppose him he had no mercy; his political enemies spent years in secret dungeons; and he did not hesitate on occasion to strike terror into his foes by an act of summary punishment. In particular the affair of the Tavoras, still wrapped away from the historian by terrible clouds of mystery, has invested his name with an atmosphere of horror.

On the night of September 3, 1758, as Joseph I was driving back to his palace after a love tryst, his carriage was fired upon from the shadows and the king seriously wounded. Three months later followed the arrest of the Marquis Tavora with his wife and children, the Duke of Aveiro and others, all charged with a conspiracy to assassinate the king. After a secret trial the accused were sentenced to death, the women to be beheaded, the men broken on the wheel. The sentence was carried out in public on January 3, 1759, with all the infamous ritual the law prescribed for the punishment of regicides. The secrecy surrounding the proceedings, the fact that Pombal kept in his possession the record of the trial, and the later discovery that parts of it had been destroyed, led his opponents to declare the whole conspiracy an invention of his imagination. Real or imagined there is no doubt that it served him well in his war against the Jesuits. A half-crazed Jesuit monk named Malagrida, confessor to the Tavoras, was implicated in the conspiracy and burned; and in 1759, Joseph, who was already out of patience with the Jesuits for their intrigues in his American colonies, was persuaded to banish the Order from all the dominions of the Portuguese crown.

CHARLES FREDERICK OF BADEN

The brilliant personality of Frederick the Great of Prussia has over-shadowed the fame of those lesser German princes of the eighteenth century who strove to prove themselves enlightened rulers; but from such oblivion the name of Charles Frederick of Baden, at least, deserves to be retrieved. Frederick himself declared that he respected Charles above all his princely contemporaries and Frederick's judgment of men was seldom at fault.

Among the many problems to which Charles Frederick gave his attention during his long reign—1748-1816—his agrarian reforms claimed the first place. In 1769 he wrote to the Marquis de Mirabeau, seeking advice on some vexatious questions of political economy. He was soon in regular communication not only with Mirabeau but with Dupont de Nemours as well, the latter becoming for a time a member of his council and tutor to his son. This connection with the Physiocrats encouraged Charles in his projects of reform and concentrated his attention on agriculture as the basis of national wealth.

Believing with Mirabeau that poor peasants make a poor kingdom and that serfdom was not only unjust but economically unsound, Charles Frederick determined to liberate all the serfs on his personal domains. He desired to establish as the foundation of the social and economic order in his state a contented class of small independent farmers. Technical improvements in agriculture, the introduction of new crops, and the encouragement of trade and manufacture, enabled him to promote the prosperity of Baden while maintaining peace with his neighbors. The population was increased by settlers who came from all parts of Germany, attracted by the religious toleration and the legal protection which Charles was able to assure his subjects. At the same time an intelligent fiscal system reduced the taxation, and the progress of education, and of the arts and sciences, made Baden, under Charles Frederick, one of the most prosperous and enlightened of the German states.

GUSTAVUS III OF SWEDEN (1771-1792)

The rôle of Sweden in the eighteenth century was that of a second rate power. Against a coalition of Denmark, Saxony, Russia, Prussia, Hanover, and England, not even the genius of Charles XII had been able to prevail; and the death of that defiant madman in 1718 brought the Great Northern War to a close disastrous to Sweden. The loss of her Baltic provinces was a serious blow to her prestige, but more fatal still were the constitutional changes which followed the peace. To replace the most absolute of monarchies the people substituted a government republican in all but name. The monarch became a puppet dignitary, while the four Estates, the nobles, clergy, burghers, and peasants, ruled by authority of a senate and a secret committee. With the rise of two political factions, the Hats, favorable to France, and the Caps, or pro-Russian party, Swedish politics became a pool of troubled waters for alien powers to fish in.

A sorrier pageant of partisanship, intrigue, and venality, than Stockholm presented in the mid-eighteenth century was difficult to find even in the Europe of the old régime. Governed by a fantastic constitution ("The worst conceived and most irrational that the mind of man has ever been able to devise," was Vergennes' summary of it) the Swedish state appeared to be drifting towards dissolution when a new figure came upon the scene. To Gustavus III all the world was a stage. From his efforts at the age of ten to construct a play to his assassination in masquerade costume at forty-six he was the consummate actor, and this genius for the theatrical, given scope by his exalted position, led him to dazzle the world with a display of the dramatic possibilities of kingship. He was, in Carlyle's phrase, "a *shining* sort of man," an artist in love with the kingly trade.

Gustavus was in Paris, charming the salons with his gaiety and brilliance, when the news arrived of his father's death. Delaying only long enough to conclude a secret alliance and provide for a secret pension from the French government, the prince started for Sweden.

"He is charming and talented," conceded his uncle, Frederick the Great, to whom he paid his respects in passing, "but he will need all his patience when he reaches his native land. It is a plague of a country to govern." The prophecy was soon justified. Gustavus appealed to the Estates with golden oratory to forget their differences, but the feuds remained unhealed. Convinced that a reassertion of the royal power alone could bring the discord to an end, he laid his plans for a *coup d'état*. Isolated in his palace the night the stroke was to fall, he organized an opera for the entertainment of his enemies, and while the nobles, their suspicions allayed, were congratulating him on his genius for stage management, the troops received their instructions. The next day he was master of Sweden.

To the diet which met at his orders on August 21, 1772, Gustavus spoke with a new note of authority. "The grief which fills my heart when I contemplate the unhappy condition of the fatherland," he began, "compels me to recall some bitter truths to your attention. . . . I had hoped that my persuasions would free you from the bonds which foreign gold, mutual hatreds, and venality, have drawn about you. I had hoped that the fate of other nations would have served as a warning to you. . . . But my pleas have left you unmoved, my endeavors have all been useless. I have trembled for the fate of my beloved country, and waited in silence the verdict of the nation on the conduct of its deputies. The masses of the people have likewise endured their burdens in silence, not knowing where to seek aid against so many evils, nor by what means the fatherland might be saved. Despair has spread throughout the kingdom until revolution raised its head. . . . In this crisis, when public liberty, public order, the very existence of the state, not to mention my own, were exposed to the greatest dangers, I have with the assistance of the Most High discovered a remedy for our woes. . . . I have saved my person and the kingdom without a single one of my subjects suffering the smallest hurt. . . ."

The deputies listened in silence to a rebuke the justice of which they dared not deny. But as Gustavus neared the close of his oration the note of reprimand forsook his voice and he appealed to his listeners, with all the charm and eloquence of which he knew himself a master, to turn their thoughts from the past to the Utopia of the future. "The one object I have in view, my dear subjects," he urged, "is the reëstablishment of liberty. That and only that can make you happy. When the laws are rendered incorruptible your possessions will be safe. No longer shall any restriction be laid upon honest industry, or justice be administered in partial and arbitrary fashion. With all things working together to increase the general prosperity, a spirit of harmony will develop in town and country. Each citizen shall be left free to enjoy what is his without let or hindrance, and we shall see reborn among us a new spirit of brotherhood, a pure piety purged of all hypocrisy and all superstition."

Such was the brilliant promise with which Gustavus inaugurated a new régime. Clothed with ample powers by a revised constitution he ruled for twenty years as

an enlightened despot. Under his direction the department of justice was purged and reorganized and the
use of torture abolished. Religious toleration, freedom
of the press, reduction of the tariff on flour and other
oppressive tolls, improvements in agriculture, in education, and in the fiscal system were further triumphs of
his reign. Yet not all the benefits conferred by a
benevolent despot could make the nobles forget their
loss of power. Their resentment deepened with the
passing years until the opposition of the parliament, or
Riksdag, of 1786 drove Gustavus to assume dictatorial
authority. Despite the open treachery of a large part
of his army he fought Russia from 1788 to 1790 and
concluded an honorable peace. His matchless oratory
secured him a final triumph over the *Riksdag* of 1792
but it was his last. On March 16 an anonymous letter
warned him that his assassination was set for that
night. A presentiment of death by violence had often
troubled him and he regarded March as his most inaus-
picious month; but perhaps he reminded himself that
the Ides of March were past, for he thrust the letter
into his pocket with a faint smile and refused all precautions. At a masquerade held the same evening in
the Opera House he was surrounded by a group of
conspirators in black dominos and shot in the back.
He died a few days later.

Among the sovereigns of the eighteenth century
Gustavus III deserves a leading place. His versatile
and lively mind enabled him to organize and electrify
every department of administration and his energetic
foreign policy all but regained for Sweden that position

among the Great Powers which the Northern War had cost her. His reign is known in Swedish history as the Gustavan Era; the Academy of Arts and Sciences owes its existence to his initiative, and the Swedish theatre some of its most charming dramas to his pen. To artists he was a Mæcenas, or rather, since the writers of the eighteenth century delighted to pursue their classical analogies, he was the Northern Augustus. But his death provided them with an even better parallel. *C. J. Cæsari virtutibus,* runs the inscription to his collected writings, *et fato similis:* like unto C. J. Cæsar in his virtues and in his fate.

STRUENSEE IN DENMARK-NORWAY

Not even the decrepit Dano-Norwegian state,[1] lying on the outskirts of Europe and consecrated to decay, was destined to escape in the eighteenth century the rough hand of the reformer. Of enlightened monarchs, it is true, the Danish annals of the period make little boast. For generations Christian had succeeded Frederick and Frederick, Christian in monotonous succession, while abuses multiplied until there was little if anything that was not rotten in the state of Denmark. Nevertheless, the early years of the reign of Christian VII (1766-1808) were marked by some daring reforms, the work not of the king (he had debauched himself to the point of imbecility) but of a royal favorite, Johan Frederick Struensee.

[1] The crowns of Denmark and Norway were united from 1397 until 1814.

From the dignity of court physician Struensee rose in favor until he became chief councillor of the incapable king and the queen's acknowledged lover. A kingdom had become his plaything and ambition urged him to essay the rôle of enlightened despot. To clear his way he swept aside the antiquated Council of State and reorganized the departments of government, removing from power any officials who ventured to oppose his projects. Between March, 1771, and January, 1772, over a thousand cabinet orders flowed from his pen, orders which left few Danish institutions undisturbed. Many of the reforms were sound in principle and highly beneficial in their effects as a short summary of the most important must indicate; but Struensee's drastic methods of procedure and his disregard of criticism angered an increasing number of the Danish people.

To the ranks of his enemies were soon added a host of ex-officials, driven from their sinecures by the rigid economy of his fiscal policy. Undeterred by their protests Struensee held his course until he had reduced the finances to order and balanced the budget. With the same thoroughness he overhauled the judicial system, abolished torture, and revised and ameliorated the penal code. All classes were promised the benefits of equality before the law, religious toleration, promotion on a basis of merit, free labor and free trade. To meet the problems of sanitation and public health, which held for him with his physician's training a particular interest, Struensee instituted a system of hospitals and

clinics, and a program of public hygiene, unique in
eighteenth century Europe.

The presumption of this minister who acted with the
insolence of a royal despot but lacked the divinity that
doth hedge a king invited a counter-stroke on the part
of his foes. It came in January, 1772. Christian VII,
liberated from a tutelage that had become virtually an
imprisonment, was persuaded to sign an order for the
arrest of his chief minister, and Struensee was seized
in his sleep. Two months later he paid for his usurpa-
tion of power on the block; but although the reaction-
aries annulled his decrees they could not altogether
undo his work. His reforms had broken through the
entrenchments of the old régime in Denmark and
opened the way for new influences and new ideas. It
was a virtue of many ideals of the Enlightenment that
they persisted on their own merits even when their
advocates perished.

TURGOT IN FRANCE

It is a fact not without irony that while French
philosophers were instructing all the princes of Europe
in statecraft, their own government remained a strong-
hold of privilege, incompetence and corruption.
Throughout the eighteenth century the prestige of the
French monarchy continued to decline at home and
abroad. Louis XV (1715-1774) forsook the business
of state for his mistresses and his masquerades; to the
warnings of his ministers that the monarchy was drifting to destruction he is credited with the reply that

the machine would last out his day and after him the deluge. So the French peasantry continued to groan beneath the burdens of an obsolete feudal tenure, while at Paris a gay and extravagant court dazzled the eyes of Europe with the brilliance of decay.

The accession of Louis XVI (1774-1793) was hailed throughout France as an omer of better days. "Any novelty," Frederick the Great observed cynically, "is popular with the French." But when the new monarch appointed as his Comptroller General the honest and courageous Turgot even the Prussian king was impressed. "I have heard high praise of M. Turgot," he wrote D'Alembert. "They say he is a man, wise, honest, and industrious. So much the better for your poor peasants. If he has a heart in his breast he will lighten the burden of their taxes." For twenty months Turgot fought to reform the administration until a combination of the Church, the *Parlement,* and the nobles overthrew him. His fall sealed the fate of the French monarchy. All possibility of a peaceful revolution having failed, it became merely a matter of time until a popular insurrection should break the yoke of privilege.

The Nemesis of the monarchy, and the final cause of its destruction, was insolvency. Turgot's proclamation on taking charge of the finances: "No bankruptcy, no increase of taxation, no loans," was a bold attempt to face this problem squarely. One expedient and one alone could render his program practicable, and that was a drastic reduction of expenditures. Any attempt at retrenchment, however, was certain to stir up such a cloud of parasites as would darken the sun. "There is no abuse that does not give some one a livelihood," Turgot wrote; and he knew that his only defence against his enemies would be the dubious buckler of the king's favor. He has been accused of forcing through his reforms with too great impetuosity; but none knew so well as he how precarious his tenure of office might prove. "Give me five years of despotism," is the prayer attributed to him, "and France shall be free." He was destined to have scarcely twenty months.

To the list of malcontents caused by the abridgment of sinecures and curtailment of pensions were soon added more powerful foes. The queen, Marie Antoinette, resented the limitations Turgot sought to impose on her expenditures; the Church feared his efforts on behalf of religious toleration; and the *Parlement* of Paris, recalled despite Turgot's protest in 1774, reasserted its ancient right of obstructing legislation. Fortune herself appeared unfavorable, for the decree establishing the freedom of the wheat trade which Turgot, true to his physiocratic principles, had made one of his first concerns, was followed by rioting and famine. To the measures which he urged upon the king for the suppression of the rioters Louis gave firm assent; but the outbreak of disturbances caused apparently by the radical legislation of the new minister damaged the latter's prestige. Admirers, who a few months earlier had hailed Turgot as a Solon about to introduce a new age of gold, began to question the wisdom of his measures; and the king himself, not for the first time, was visited by doubts.

On January 5, 1776, Turgot laid before the Royal Council six edicts embodying the reforms which he considered most imperative. Four of the decrees involved fiscal proposals of a secondary importance; but two—the abolition of the *corvée* and the suppression of the trade-guilds—were revolutionary in their implications. The *corvée* was a method of forced labor whereby the peasants were compelled to spend twelve to fifteen days a year repairing the roads, a service from which the nobility and gentry derived the chief advantage. Turgot planned to convert this compulsory labor into a tax or money payment, and had he proposed to levy the assessment only on those classes of citizens subject to the *corvée* he might have carried his point. His aim, however, as he frankly stated, was to assess the nobility and clergy, hitherto exempt from such taxes, on an equal basis with the peasants. To a decree which challenged their immunity in so audacious a fashion the privileged classes registered an implacable opposition.

The edict for the suppression of the trade-guilds drew upon Turgot denunciations no less bitter from members of the bourgeoisie. These guilds, which dated for the most part from the Middle Ages, were exclusive industrial corporations, unsuited to the economic conditions of the eighteenth century. The masters of a guild, possessing a monopoly in the manufacture and sale of various necessary commodities, could enrich themselves at the expense of the public welfare. Furthermore, their statutes authorized them to limit the number of workers engaged in a trade, and to prevent an artisan, however skilled, from practising his profession unless he were a guild member. All these restrictions and privileges Turgot attempted to sweep away in a single edict. The guilds, he insisted, must be dissolved; workmen were to be left free to practise whatever trade they wished; and any union of masters, journeymen, or apprentices was to be held illegal.

When the *Parlement* refused to register the Six Edicts Turgot appealed to the king. Accordingly, at a *lit de justice* held March 12, 1776, Louis went through the ceremony of appearing before the *Parlement* in person and commanding the chamber to register the decrees. The *Parlement*, according to accepted precedent, had no course but to comply; refusal would have had no effect save perhaps to draw upon the members a sentence of exile to their country estates. At the end of five hours the last decree had been read and accepted, but Turgot's triumph was a hollow one. His influence, already undermined, had been strained too far by this display of authority; his only shield was the king's favor and Louis chose this moment to abandon him. Refusing to recognize that his ministry was over Turgot wrote the king again and again begging him to awe the rebellious *Parlement* into a proper submission and dare to carry out the necessary reforms. "Do not forget, Sire," he counselled, "it was weakness that brought the head of Charles I to the block. . . ." But Louis avoided a meeting with his Comptroller General, and when he finally wrote him on May 12 it was to request his resignation. Forced into retirement Turgot had to watch in silence the exultation of his enemies and the annulment of his decrees. He died in 1781; had he survived a few years longer he might have witnessed the bloody triumph of Liberty, Equality, and Fraternity, and mourned the death of the irresolute king his prescience could not save.

FROM REFORM TO REVOLUTION

Through a study of the enlightened despots and their reforms it becomes evident that European institutions in the eighteenth century were everywhere in need of renovation. The general similarity of the various reform programs, and the fact that they were supported by a consistent philosophy, prove that enlightened men in each country recognized the prevalent evils and were in substantial agreement as to the best remedies to apply to them. The one point about which some uncertainty persisted was the question to whom the task of remodelling society might most happily be entrusted.

Upon the answer vouchsafed to this question depended the difference between reform and revolution. For when political innovations are undertaken by an existing government on its own behalf they are known as reforms; when they are introduced in defiance of the government and lead to its overthrow they constitute a revolution. In general the political thinkers of the eighteenth century favored the method of reform. They endorsed monarchy as the most satisfactory type of government and they regarded a despot as peculiarly fitted to carry through the reform program. The monarchs for the most part were ready to undertake this duty. Could they have secured the whole-hearted support of their subjects they might have reconstructed the old régime and adapted its institutions to meet newer requirements. To a certain extent this is what did happen in Sweden, in Spain, in Austria, and in Prussia.

Yet the far-reaching alterations which the time demanded, even when carried out by royal authority, were none the less revolutionary in their scope. The enlightened despots by their reforming zeal set a dangerous example to their subjects. Their legislative experiments when successful taught the people to desire better government; when they failed they left a deepened consciousness of existing evils. More effectively than the *philosophes* these monarchs taught contempt for privilege and tradition. Their ruthless suppression or modification of established institutions—of the Church, the feudal courts, the trade-guilds—dispelled the veneration with which men had regarded these august survivals of medievalism. It is difficult to tear down part of a building without endangering the rest. When so many ancient institutions were being weighed in the balance and found wanting, monarchy also was certain sooner or later to be faced with the ordeal of justifying itself before the bar of rationalism. This menace was implicit in the reform philosophy from the first but it is only when it proclaimed itself in a manner rude and unmistakable that the reform movement can be dignified with the name of revolution. The refusal of the French Estates General in 1789 to disband "until they had given France a constitution" was a direct challenge to a despotic monarchy and thus marks the opening of the revolutionary era.

As reflected in philosophical speculation (the philosophy of the eighteenth century was a pool in which coming events cast their shadows before) the transition from reform to revolution may be discerned with the publication of Rousseau's *Social Contract* in 1761. By his insistence that sovereignty resides not with the monarch but with the people Rousseau suggested a counter authority by which reforms might be invoked and executed; a substitute horse as it were that might be yoked to the reform chariot. The theories of the Social Contract and Popular Sovereignty reduced a king and his ministers to the status of magistrates responsible to the people, and liable, if they failed in their duties, to be relieved of their delegated authority. "What we have said," Rousseau wrote in summing up the obligations of a ruler to his subjects, ". . . makes it clear . . . that the depositaries of the executive power are not the people's masters, but its officers; that it can set them up and pull them down when it likes; that for them there is no question of contract, but of obedience; and that in taking charge of the functions the State imposes on them they are doing no more than fulfilling their duty as citizens, without having the remotest right to argue about the conditions."

In the eighteenth century, France, alone of the larger European nations, failed to experience the benefits of enlightened despotism. Disabused in consequence of the temptation to put their trust in princes the French people were the first to cast about for a different solu-

tion to their difficulties.   The reforms—establishment
of civil equality and religious toleration, destruction of
privileges, of trade restrictions, of feudal dues, of serfdom—which in other countries were attempted singlehanded by the sovereign princes, in France, when all
other efforts had failed, were carried through by the
authority of the sovereign people.

BIBLIOGRAPHICAL NOTE

The following works are listed as useful suggestions for students who may desire further reading on any of the major topics introduced in this study.

GENERAL WORKS

The Cambridge Modern History. Volume VI. New York, 1909. The general excellence of this work and its accessibility make it of prime importance. References to individual chapters are given below in connection with particular topics.

Johnson, Arthur Henry. *The Age of the Enlightened Despot, 1660-1789.* London, 1925. This is a good general treatment of the despots and their policies.

Bourne, Henry Eldridge. *The Revolutionary Period in Europe (1763-1815).* New York, 1914. Chapters ii, iv, and v discuss in an interesting manner the attempts at reform under the old régime.

Lowell, Edward Jackson. *The Eve of the French Revolution,* Boston, 1892. This is still one of the best discussions of the social and political conditions which the enlightened despots sought to remedy and which finally brought about the revolution.

WORKS ON PARTICULAR SUBJECTS

The Philosophy of the Eighteenth Century

Robertson, John Mackinnon. *A Short History of Free Thought,* 3rd revised edition, 2 Volumes, New York,

1915. Volume II, chapter xvi, contains a scholarly and sympathetic discussion of deism and rationalism in the eighteenth century.

Higgs, Henry. *The Physiocrats*, London, 1897. This is one of the best short studies on the Physiocrats and their influence.

The Catholic Church

Barry, William. *The Papacy and Modern Times, A Political Sketch, 1303-1870.* Home University Library. New York, 1911. Chapter iii includes the founding of the Jesuit Order; chapter v affords a splendid short account of the political history of the Church in the eighteenth century and the suppression of the Jesuits.

Frederick the Great of Prussia

Reddaway, William Fiddian. *Frederick the Great and the Rise of Prussia.* ("Heroes of the Nations" Series) New York, 1904. This is one of the best short biographies in English.

Henderson, Ernest Flagg. *A Short History of Germany,* new revised edition, New York, 1916. Chapter iv on "The Wars of Frederick the Great," and chapter v on "Frederick the Great in Time of Peace" give an excellent picture of this monarch.

Koser, Reinhold. *Geschichte Friedrichs des Grossen,* 5th edition, 4 Volumes, Stuttgart, 1912-14. This is the most authoritative and scholarly life of Frederick that has been published.

The Emperor Joseph II

Bright, James Franck. *Joseph II.* ("Foreign Statesmen" Series.) London, 2nd edition, 1905. This biography is a sequel to the author's *Maria Theresa,* published in the same series, 1897.

Coxe, William. *History of the House of Austria, 1218 to*

1792. 3rd edition, 3 Volumes, London, 1847. (Bohn's
Standard Library.) This work though somewhat antiquated is still excellent. The third volume offers
what is perhaps the best account in English of the
reigns of Joseph II and Leopold II.

Mitrofanov, Paul v. *Joseph II. Seine politische und kul-
turelle Tätigheit.* Translated from the Russian into
German by V. v. Demelič. 2 Volumes, Vienna, 1910.
An indispensable work for any student desiring to
understand the significance of Joseph's reform projects.

Cambridge Modern History, Volume VI, chapter xviii, is an
able short account of Joseph's reign.

Catharine the Great of Russia

Hodgetts, E. A. Brayley. *The Life of Catharine the Great
of Russia,* New York, 1914. A popular but not uncrit-
ical biography of Catharine in English.

Cambridge Modern History, Volume VI, chapter xix.

Poland

Bain, Robert Nisbet. *The Last King of Poland and His
Contemporaries,* New York, 1909. Traces the decadence of the Polish kingdom in the eighteenth century,
the first partition in 1772, attempts at reconstruction,
and the final dismemberment, 1792-95.

Charles III of Spain

Rousseau, François. *Règne de Charles III d'Espagne,
1759-1788.* 2 Volumes, Paris, 1907. The most ex-
haustive work on this subject.

Cambridge Modern History, Volume VI, chapter xii.

Pombal in Portugal

Stephens, Henry Morse. *Portugal.* ("Story of the Nations"
Series), New York, 1903. Chapter xvi offers a clear
short account of Portuguese history in the eighteenth

century, the reforms of Pombal, and the expulsion of the Jesuits.

Gustavus III of Sweden

Bain, Robert Nisbet. *Gustavus III and His Contemporaries, 1746-1792.* 2 Volumes. London, 1894. A brilliant biography of a brilliant monarch.

Cambridge Modern History, Volume VI, chapter xxi, by the same author as the above.

Struensee in Denmark

Bain, Robert Nisbet. *Scandinavia. A Political History of Denmark, Norway and Sweden from 1513 to 1900.* Cambridge Historical Series. New York, 1905. Chapter xv contains an able discussion of Struensee's reforms. There is no life of Struensee in English.

Cambridge Modern History, Volume VI, chapter xxi, is devoted to Denmark in the latter half of the eighteenth century.

Turgot in France

Say, Jean Baptiste Léon. *Turgot.* Translated by Melville B. Anderson. Chicago, 1888. A valuable short analysis of Turgot's policies by a famous French economist.

INDEX